Embrace the Cross

Books by Chip Brogden

Strength for the Journey
Why Do You Call Me Lord?
Infinite Supply
The Ekklesia
The Irresistible Kingdom
The Irresistible Life
Getting Babylon Out of You

A CALL TO RADICAL DISCIPLESHIP

EMBRACE
the
CROSS

CHIP BROGDEN

All Scripture quotations, unless otherwise noted, are from the Holy Bible, English Standard Version, copyright ©2001 by Crossway Bibles, a division of Good News Publishers. Used by permission. All rights reserved.

Scripture quotations marked (NLT) are taken from the Holy Bible, New Living Translation, copyright ©1996. Used by permission of Tyndale House Publishers Inc., Wheaton, Illinois 60189. All rights reserved.

Scripture quotations marked (TIL) are taken from *The Irresistible Life*, a paraphrase of the Gospel of John, copyright ©2008 by Chip Brogden. Used by permission. All rights reserved.

Embrace the Cross
©2009 Chip Brogden

Printed in the United States of America. All rights reserved under International Copyright Law. Contents may no be reproduced in whole or in part without the express written consent of the publisher.

Published by The School of Christ
http://www.TheSchoolOfChrist.Org

Contents

Preface — xi

1. Back to the Cross — 13
2. The Call of the Cross — 25
3. The Hidden Wisdom — 45
4. No Good Thing — 61
5. The Need for Brokenness — 75
6. The Secret of Spiritual Power — 95
7. Crucified With Christ — 107
8. The Two-Fold Work of the Cross — 131
9. The Prisoners of the Lord — 139
10. The Way of the Cross — 153
11. Embrace the Cross — 163

The Next Step — 191

Preface

The essays in this book were written at various times over the course of a decade, between 1999 and 2009. For our family, these ten years have been the most difficult of our lives, as well as the most *joyful*. The depth of your revelation is measured by the depth of your suffering. Such is the way of the Cross, a way that we have witnessed time and again as the means through which God intends to *reduce us to Christ*.

As I look back on this time now, seeing "both the goodness and the severity of God" (Rom. 11:22), I recall the words of Corrie Ten Boom: "You may never know that Jesus is all you *need* until Jesus is all you *have*." We know it now. I trust you know it too, or will soon.

Rest assured that the truths presented in this book are not mere theories, but have been tested in the crucible of actual experience. We pray something written here will encourage and challenge both "saints and sinners" alike to count the cost, embrace the Cross, grow up spiritually, and know Jesus as you have never known Him before.

Chip Brogden
Canandaigua, N.Y.
November, 2009

"The cross is the symbol of Christianity, and the cross speaks of death and separation, never of compromise. No one ever compromised with a cross. The cross separated between the dead and the living.

"The timid and the fearful will cry 'Extreme!' and they will be right. The cross is the essence of all that is extreme and final."

~ A. W. Tozer

Chapter One

Back to the Cross

"For I decided to know nothing among you except Jesus Christ and him crucified." (1 Corinthians 2:2)

Though Paul had quite a bit of knowledge and many things to say and teach the Corinthians, he determined to become a man of one subject: Jesus Christ, and Him crucified.

We must become foolish in order to be wise.

We must give up everything in order to get back everything.

We must become weak in order to be strong.

We must die in order to live.

We can quote these teachings of Jesus, seek to imitate Him as our Example, strive to walk the narrow Way, and even accomplish many good deeds in His Name. But apart from the Cross these activities are wood, hay and stubble. The moment we are challenged or confronted by the opposition we will fall away. Perhaps we can appear to be patient, but a day comes when we lose our patience. Perhaps we can appear to be gentle, but a day comes when our roughness is revealed. Perhaps we can appear to be humble, but a day comes when pride is discovered in us and we fall. Perhaps we can obey the letter of the law and appear outwardly to others as being righteous, but when alone and faced with the secrets of our heart and mind, we discover that the inside of the cup is full of uncleanness.

In calling us to come back to the Cross, God is asking us to lay down our lives and embrace the Wisdom of death, burial, resurrection, and ascension in order to live as sons and daughters within the Kingdom of God. Apart from the Cross we can neither enter the Kingdom nor live in the Spirit, no matter how great the desire. Apart from the Cross we do not know what it is to turn the other cheek, to go the extra mile, to love our enemies, or to pray for those who persecute us. Apart from the Cross we do not know what it is to submit to the will of God, accept suffering, and cast ourselves upon Him. Apart from the Cross we cannot know what Resurrection is.

Religion seeks to reform a man; the Cross seeks to crucify him. Religion may fail to bring about the desired result, but the Cross never fails to achieve its end. Mankind will pursue morality, virtue, spirituality, and even perform religious works and good deeds in order to avoid death on the Cross. But there are no wounds, no scars, no evidence of having ever died and been made alive unto God. Either a man has never died, or he has died and been raised to Life. You cannot fake a resurrection.

The Cross is the means by which God reduces us to Christ, that we may be raised to new Life. What cannot be accomplished in a lifetime of self-effort is easily accomplished in God through the Cross. We may take many shortcuts along the way and attempt to escape the inevitable, but the day we cease striving and meekly accept the Cross we find everything is done for us. In fact, death by crucifixion cannot be accomplished by suicide. We cannot crucify ourselves. The instrument of our death is chosen for us, as well as the manner in which it is carried out. The timing and the duration of the execution – all is controlled by Another. There is nothing to be done, for we must submit to the Unseen Hand and cast ourselves completely upon Him.

If we will follow Jesus, we must take up the Cross daily, deny ourselves, and follow Him (Lk. 9:23).

The Cross Is Wisdom Through Foolishness

> For the word of the cross is folly to those who are perishing, but to us who are being saved it is the power of God. (1 Cor. 1:18a)

There is a wisdom which comes from above. This wisdom is counter to the wisdom which is earthly. Our thoughts, reasonings, arguments, rationales, and opinions are worthless in God's sight. We are commanded to have the mind of Christ and to seek the Wisdom which comes from God.

Humanly speaking, the Cross makes no sense. If we approach God with only our minds then we will never know Him. If we study the Cross in order to gain a new teaching or doctrine, it will make no impression on us. Indeed, we may memorize the appropriate verses of Scripture, even teach others what we have learned, and never experience the reality of it. How easily and freely we may talk about dying to Self, taking up the Cross, and living the crucified life. But knowledge without experience is nothing. Indeed, knowledge without experience only deceives us into thinking we are living something just because we are able to rehearse a few facts mentally. This counts for nothing in spiritual matters.

We must ask God to empty us of our preconceived ideas and notions and fill us instead with His Mind. We must relinquish our wisdom and receive His Wisdom. His Wisdom is how *He* sees things. How we see things is irrelevant, and will mislead us. His Ways and His Mind are higher than our ways and our mind. The Cross is the means by which God seeks to destroy our earthly wisdom and our carnal mind. The Cross, then, is wisdom through foolishness.

The Cross Is Gaining Through Losing

In order to accumulate more, we usually think that we must add to that which we have already. The Wisdom of God teaches us that in order to gain, you must first lose. Think of a child who refuses to let go of his old, broken toys in order to receive new ones from his father. To his mind he is losing something. But by letting go, by giving up, he gains.

Like the child, we stubbornly refuse to relinquish our grip on our spiritual possessions. We tenaciously cling to things as a child would cling to a collection of broken toys. We collect teachings, experiences, and good deeds, pointing to these as proof that we are spiritually endowed. Until we are willing to part with our "riches" we will not be able to receive the true Riches of Christ in us. The Cross demonstrates that we do not gain by trying to get, but by losing in order to gain. We cannot really receive from God until we have learned to give up to God. It is the spirit which cries, "Not my will, but Yours be done" and "Father, into Your Hand I commit my spirit."

These words are easily uttered, but we cannot appreciate them or really experience them until we have been through our Gethsemane experiences and our Golgotha experiences. Until that time we are merely reciting some words, but we do not truly know what it means to give ourselves up to God, or to be completely consecrated and submitted to Him. The Cross prepares us to receive by first forcing us to give up. Therefore, the Cross is gaining through losing.

The Cross Is Power Through Weakness

> But God chose what is foolish in the world to shame the wise; God chose what is weak in the world to shame the strong. (1 Cor. 1:27b)

To the natural way of thinking, power and weakness are opposites. That is, in order to have power, we must eliminate weakness. The Wisdom of God teaches us differently. This Wisdom tells us that the weak things are chosen to overcome the mighty things, and power works concurrently with weakness.

The Cross is meant to inflict pain, weaken, and slowly kill. It is the ultimate expression of weakness. The victim is stripped naked and nailed to the wood through their hands and feet. Their weight is supported by their legs until they are too tired to stand. When their legs give way their entire weight is supported by their outstretched arms (to speed this process along the legs are sometimes broken). The chest cavity is eventually pulled apart from this stress and the helpless victim slowly dies of suffocation as the lungs collapse.

The crucified one can hardly move, much less struggle. Once the nails are in place there is no way to remove them. You carry nothing with you, and have nothing remaining. You can neither speed up nor slow down your death. The shame of your nakedness is open for all to see. Besides the physical suffering, the soul is stripped of its dignity and pride. There is no escape.

God desires to give you power, but that power only comes through weakness. Any power not obtained through weakness is illegitimate, no matter how spiritual it appears. The only legitimate power is granted to those who have been made weak. Power is birthed in weakness. Many exude a certain "power" but there is not the corresponding weakness. Hence, the power only gives them an occasion for boasting. To remedy this, God has ordained that all who would have His power must first be weakened and made empty – we refer to this as being "broken." The purpose of weakness and suffering is to open the way for His Power. The instrument that God uses to weaken us is the Cross. Therefore, the Cross is power through weakness.

The Cross Is Life Through Death

> I have been crucified with Christ. It is no longer I who live, but Christ who lives in me. (Gal. 2:20a)

There can be no Resurrection Life without a Crucified Death. Naturally we expect that in order to live we must avoid death at all costs. Yet, the Wisdom of God teaches us that Life is found by embracing Death – that is, as we die to ourselves and embrace the Cross, we are made alive in Christ.

There is a principle of death that works in us. As soon as we are born, we begin to age and die. For the person who is in Christ, physical death is not the end, but the beginning. Likewise, a God-ordained death on the Cross is not the end, but the beginning. The Cross works death in us that the Spirit may work Life in us. The Cross kills that which needs to be killed in us, whereas the Spirit gives New Life. The Cross beats and tears down, while the Spirit rebuilds. Only those who have experienced Death can truly minister Life and speak to dead men.

Now, if we have not learned what it is to die daily, we will not experience the Life of God daily. In a word, I am dead; yet I am living. I am crucified, yet I am alive. On the one hand I am weakened to the point of death and am powerless; on the other hand, I live by the power of God and am strengthened with all might by His Spirit Who lives in me. The moment I cease to experience death, however, at that precise moment I cease to experience Life, for the Cross is Life through death.

The Aim of God's Dealings

> "Do you want to know the truth? The truth is that when you were young, you could dress yourself and go wherever you wanted to go. But when you are older, you too, will stretch out your hands and Someone Else will clothe you and tell you where to go." (Jn. 21:18, TIL)

Though our heart attitude should be childlike, God desires us to be mature men and women. He desires us to grow spiritually. In order to accomplish this He allows us to meet with many disagreeable circumstances and trials.

When we are young in the Lord we do as we please. We find much pleasure in serving the Lord according to our own thought, and everything is light and carefree. We live a life of feeling and sensation. We are easily moved by how we feel. If we are happy, we gladly deny ourselves and pour ourselves out in service. But when we are sad or troubled by our circumstances, we feel as though we have been deserted. The Lord must then reach forth and draw the little sheep back to Himself again, whereupon our feeling is restored and we renew our devotion with the same vigor as before. This is the way of those who are young: they dress themselves and go where they wish.

But when we are older in the Lord, the life of faith commences as we stretch forth our hands in surrender and allow Another to dress us and carry us where we do not wish to go. We no longer dress ourselves and go our own way. We no longer walk, but we are carried. We may no longer consider our own wishes. We may no longer act according to a will of our own apart from God's will. Instead, we have finally submitted to God's dealings with us. We recognize at last how until now we have been full of ourselves: speaking many words in addition to what God had given us, and performing many acts apart from the ones that God was calling us to perform. Likewise, we see how often we have failed to speak and act on many occasions because we simply loved ourselves more than we loved God.

This transition between a life of feeling and a life of faith, from being self-ruled to being Spirit-ruled, does not happen in a few days. What stands between the experience of the young and the experience of the old? What is it that brings about this maturity? How is this growth achieved? By what means does God accomplish this work of transformation? In speaking to Peter, the Lord is telling him by what death he will die to glorify God (v.19). We know that Peter was eventually crucified upside-down and died a martyr's death. But the *daily Cross* of self-denial that Peter bore was the means by which God was able to subdue his wild nature and transform him into a man of faith. He was a living sacrifice. The physical cross upon which he died was a testimony to his having already laid down his life a million times prior to that final act.

The death God really seeks in us is not the future laying down of our physical life, but the moment-by-moment laying down of our Self. It is not the once-and-for-all martyr's death, but the daily dying and living unto God that brings Him the most glory. In fact, those who have not denied themselves in the seemingly insignificant matters of daily life will find it difficult, if not impossible, to lay down their physical lives should that be required of them.

God is calling us to become foolish in order to be wise; to give up everything in order to get back everything; to become weak in order to become strong; to come back to the Cross and die that we may live. In these pages we hope to communicate this urgent call. Today, let us ask God to quicken this to our hearts, and grant that we may become People of the Cross, experiencing the Death of the Lord that we may have the Life of the Lord. Let us determine from now on to know nothing, but Christ and Him crucified: for "A disciple is not above his teacher, but everyone when he is fully trained will be like his teacher" (Lk. 6:40).

"Jesus tapped me on the shoulder and said, 'Bob, why are you resisting me?' I said, 'I'm not resisting you!' He said, 'You gonna follow me?' I said, 'I've never thought about that before!' He said, 'When you're not following me, you're resisting me.'"

~ Bob Dylan

Chapter Two

The Call of the Cross

"Whoever does not take his cross and follow me is not worthy of me." (Matthew 10:38)

Are you worthy of the Lord Jesus Christ?
　Hear what the Lord is saying here. "If you do not take up your Cross and follow Me, you do not deserve Me." It is not merely a question of whether or not we are following Christ. The crux of the matter is: have we taken up the Cross? There is an order to this call to become disciples of Jesus Christ. First we must take up our Cross and only then may we follow after Him. It is not, "First follow Me, and later take up your Cross." Taking up your Cross is the first step.

　Our taking up the Cross is basic to our following Christ; not something we are called to do after many years. The so-called "deeper Christian life" is but the normal Christian life. Anything less is abnormal. There is no greater depth to the Christian life but what God expects of all of us from the beginning. If we are getting any "deeper" it is only because we have been shallow until now. We must take up our Cross and follow Jesus.

　If I am to take up the Cross it not only signifies my willingness to die, but my actual death. The Cross is not theoretical, but very real. Being willing to die is good, but actually dying and then living again is best. To take up the Cross today is to accept the sentence of death today. It is the beginning of the end of my life. The Cross does not merely weaken me, but kills me. Some believe that all is well because they are willing to die for their faith. This is not good enough for Jesus Christ. Many radical religious activists strap explosive devices to themselves and blow up innocent people and buildings because of their faith. Clearly they are deceived by a false sense of duty – yet they are more dedicated to their religion than their Christian counterparts are to their Lord. Faith is not following Christ and then dying, but dying first and then following. Here the demands of Christ far exceed those of other religions. Christ bids us to die, and *then* follow.

Some will say, "I am willing to die now that I have followed." The person who knows the Cross says, "I am fit to follow now that I have died." Why is this important? Because Jesus knows that no human being is qualified to follow Him until they have first died. Jesus knows a man cannot live until he has died and been raised to Life. He therefore asks us to die right away, that He may raise us from the dead by His Spirit living in us and then He will place us immediately upon the correct path.

A Common Experience

What is the experience of many Christians? They are taught to come to the Lord just as they are, right away, and allow Him to save them. Then they are instructed to read the Bible, pray, attend church services, pay their tithes, and witness for Christ. But to their great surprise, it is most difficult for them to forsake sin. Even after many years of faithful activity not a few of them still struggle with the same besetting sins. Or, even if they are able through force of will or peer pressure to lay aside the outward sins, they are seemingly powerless to overcome their own inward condition.

Pride, gossip, jealousy, self-righteousness, intolerance – many saints are struggling with these things many years after they first begin to follow the Lord, even if they have forsaken their more "physical" vices. And if we look closely enough we will sometimes find that even these obvious "sins of the flesh" are still present, often against their will and in spite of many attempts to forsake their lusts. Yet they cannot overcome them. In a word, some positive changes notwithstanding, the Christian's life is frequently one of many ups and downs – a few victories sprinkled in amongst many defeats, a cycle of trying, failing, and trying again; continually striving against sin.

If counseling is sought, the Christian in such a situation is basically told to gird up their loins yet again and redouble their efforts in prayer, Bible study, and church attendance. They are encouraged to confess their sins and keep trying. A new book promises to give them the secret of the Christian life, and they eagerly read the book and put some of it to good use for a time, but this too fails to provide a lasting solution to their chronic condition. Or maybe it is a new teaching tape, or a different church. Or perhaps a new emphasis on a particular teaching, be it spiritual warfare, prayer, or worship. If fasting is believed to be the answer, then fast they will, but not with any lasting results. They may even hear the message of self-denial and voice their amen to it. They resolve to die and deny themselves. But the more they try to die, the more alive they become.

For many years this was my experience. I first prayed to the Lord at the age of eight, and then sought to live a Christian life out of my own efforts. I remember when I was just a boy of thirteen years old, I determined to go to school and live without sinning that entire day. You would think such a task was comparatively easy for a boy, but I found myself to be sinning almost before school started! My thoughts, my words, my actions, all rose up to condemn me. At the end of the day I could only pray for forgiveness and resolve to do better tomorrow. Yet I again met with failure. Just as I was sure that victory was mine, I would fall – and it was not even 9:00! By lunchtime I had given up, and by evening I was confessing my sins again and resolving to do better the next day. Through the years I have counseled and prayed with enough Christians to know that my experience is neither unusual nor unique, and is common to saints of all ages and backgrounds.

What is the problem here? It is simply this: we attempt to follow before we have died. It is unfortunate that after many years of service the Lord still has to call us back to the Cross, yet this is precisely where we should have begun.

Although we ought to encourage people to come as they are and trust the Lord for salvation, we must also teach them that they must count the cost and take up the Cross: otherwise they are not worthy of Jesus! God cannot fill us until He empties us. The Cross is where we are poured out that He may pour in. Unfortunately, salvation as preached today results not in death, but in "swooning." There is an ecstatic joy and the "near death experience" of a token surrender, but it is not real death. The convert merely changes his conduct, cries a few tears, yet he still lives. The outward deportment may be different, but he has not died. He commences to follow the Lord and fill his life with religious activity, but his many failures and shortcomings prove something is missing in his experience.

What is missing? He knows the cross only as something Jesus died on for him. The cross does not represent his own death, but his Lord's death. It is seldom presented as anything other than the means of atonement and forgiveness of sins. Few realize it is the means by which we enter, as well as live, the Christian life.

Following Christ Versus Taking Up The Cross

May God give us spiritual vision to see the multitudes who claim to be following Christ today. If we were to pick one of these followers out of the crowd and ask if they were truly following the Lord, they would probably say yes. If we were to ask how they knew they were following Christ, they would likely point to a time in which they prayed the sinner's prayer and received Christ. Or they would talk about the church they attend, or their knowledge of spiritual things, or their particular ministry. It is interesting that while most Christians know that they are not saved by works, when pressed they will nevertheless point to their works as proof that they are indeed following the Lord.

Certainly we do not wish to discourage anyone from spiritual activities. Yet we maintain that it is possible to follow Christ and yet not be worthy of Him. I am not too interested in someone's ability to teach the Scriptures, faithfully attend church services, witness to strangers, build churches or display other external "evidences" of following Christ. Though well-intentioned, I only wish to know: have you taken up the Cross? Have you died? If you will but go to the Cross and die, then there is hope for you. Otherwise you are just another religious person.

People will do anything to save themselves from death on the Cross – if necessary, they will even pursue a religious, moral, ethical, and spiritual lifestyle – so long as they see it will benefit them. They do not understand that Christ will not accept those who follow Him unless they have taken up their Cross first.

Even the term "born-again" implies a death, and a re-birthing. Has this been your experience, or is it just a euphemism for "getting religious?" Some claim a born-again experience when it is clear that they have not died at all! They have received some teaching, prayed a prayer, cleaned up their life to an extent, even performed some good deeds. But any person can become religious and turn over a new moral leaf. When talking with such ones you hope to touch the Lord through them, but you come away with a sense that you touched them, and not the Lord they claim to represent. They are "alive" and their own aliveness shows through to the extent that you wonder if the Life of Christ is anywhere to be found in them. There seems to be little room for Jesus because Self remains enthroned, even in the midst of a lot of seemingly spiritual work and ministry. This explains why many will truthfully say to the Lord that they have done many mighty works in His Name, but for all that He replies, "Depart from Me; I do not know you." How can this be?

Christ does not call us to *clean up* our life, but to *give up* our life. So the issue is not if you are one of the multitudes following Christ, but rather, have you taken up the Cross? For this is the beginning of following Christ.

Not I, But Christ

What is the Christian life? It is I in Christ, and it is Christ in me and through me, doing what I cannot do myself. "I have been crucified with Christ. It is no longer I who live, but Christ who lives in me" (Gal. 2:20a). This is the secret of the Christian life. It is not girding up the loins and striving to do better – it is realizing we *cannot*, and ceasing to do, trusting Him to do what we cannot. Our problem is we think we *can* do it. Hopefully we realize we cannot save ourselves, and so we trust the Lord for that; but in everything else we ask the Lord to help us do it ourselves.

Imagine the foolishness of saying to the Lord, "Please help me to save myself. I will work very hard and do the best I can. I pray You will strengthen me." If you hear someone praying this way, hopefully you will explain to them that though they may be praying in sincerity, they are praying ignorantly. For we are not saved by trusting Christ to help us save ourselves, but by giving up trying to save ourselves and trusting Him to do what we cannot do. Once we realize it is by grace, and not works, there is nothing to do but raise our hands to heaven and say, "Lord Jesus, I cannot save myself – I trust You for that! I receive the gift of God! Thank you for saving me!" Prayer for help to do it becomes praise to God that it is already done.

But then what happens? We go forth and attempt to put into practice the teachings of Christ with our own human strength, willpower, and resolutions. That is not Christianity, that is religion. Jesus did not come to merely tell us how to live, or even to merely show us how to live. He came to be our Life. I live in union with Him, and He lives in union with me. The Teacher is one with the student. The Master is one with the disciple. Where and when do the two become one? At the Cross. This is precisely what Galatians 2:20 is saying. And please notice that it begins with, "I have been crucified with Christ." Please do not miss this. We cannot be raised with Him unless we are crucified with Him. I am dying in order for Christ to live in me. I accept the sentence of Death that I may have His Life in the place of my own. It is no longer I who lives, but Christ Who lives in me. Otherwise, such a life is completely beyond me, totally out of my reach.

You see, the problem is not my impatience, ingratitude, laziness, or pride. These are but symptoms of the problem, but the common approach is to treat the symptoms and leave the real problem – the condition which causes the symptoms - untouched. Or to put it another way, we chop off a few leaves from the tree, but the tree itself remains.

The problem is not what I *do*, but what I *am*! I may be able to change my conduct, but I cannot change who I am. Real progress occurs when I admit that I am the problem and I ask God to take the axe to the root! This was the preaching of John the Baptist. "Even now the axe is laid to the root of the trees. Every tree therefore that does not bear good fruit is cut down and thrown into the fire" (Mt. 3:10). Jesus wields the axe, and the root is the thing that makes me accept those solicitations to sin – Self. Plucking off the bad fruit is pointless. As soon as I get rid of one piece, three more spring up. When I get rid of those three, ten more come to life.

Put the axe to the root and the problem of the fruit is solved. Put the sinner to death and the problem of his sins is solved as well. May we see that the greatest enemy is not "out there" somewhere, but right here within us. As someone has said, we have seen the enemy, and it is us. So, the Cross seeks not to reform us, but to transform us through death and resurrection. God cures us by removing us from the equation altogether. Our old life is cut off and a new Seed begins to take root and bring forth spiritual fruit.

How do we live out the Christian life? It begins with taking up the Cross. Then, and only then, can we follow; for when we cease to do, He begins to do. We cannot keep our life and have His Life. Which do you want? You cannot keep His and have yours too. But this is exactly what many want. They want to go to heaven, but they also want to do as they please on earth. They want the blessings of God, but they do not want to sacrifice too much. They want to reign with Him, but they don't want to suffer with Him. They want to follow His will, but only when it agrees with their will, otherwise you will witness a mammoth struggle and see them cry many tears of self-pity. They eagerly accept the messages of power, blessings, eternal life, and spiritual gifts; but they reject the calls for self-denial, submission, surrender, and sanctification. They view the Christian life as a buffet meal in which they get to pick and choose what they want to partake of. They are firmly in control of their own lives and Christ is there to render them assistance upon request if they really get into a bind. Otherwise they do as they please and follow their own thoughts, blazing their own easy trail somewhere proximate to, but not exactly in, the Narrow Way. This accounts for their many defeats and failures as they struggle to be "good Christians."

Please know that Christ is not here to help you become a better person, but to make you so weak in yourself and so sick of your own way that you can do nothing but trust in Him to do what you at last realize you cannot do. It does not matter if that something "we cannot do" is save ourselves, control our temper, get along with others, raise our children, or overcome a lustful habit. The course is the same. After many attempts and failures we at last realize we cannot, so we throw ourselves on the mercy of God and trust Him to do what we cannot do. Just as salvation is ours through faith by grace, and not through ourselves, so it is with living the Christian life.

The difference between a defeated Christian and a victorious Christian is simply this: the former lives by his own power and asks for God's help and will almost as an afterthought, while the latter despairs of himself, lays down his life, and trusts Christ to live in his place at all times. The Cross is how God accomplishes this task of bringing us to the end of ourselves. Then we can say, "Not I, but Christ."

We surrender our lives that we may have His Life. We live the Christian life the same way in which we enter the Christian life – by admitting our inability to do anything of ourselves, and trusting in Him to do it through us. First, it is the question of salvation. Then, and for the rest of our lives, it is the question of daily living and working out our salvation. There is a world of difference between asking Christ to help me do it and trusting Him to do it through me. The difference is a matter of success and failure, victory and defeat.

How do most Christians live out their faith? They start out by grace, but quickly fall back upon works. They see Christ as helping them to live, instead of Christ as their Life. They have not died, and the harder they try, the more frustrated they become. When we finally realize that we are called to take up the Cross before we begin to follow, we see the wisdom of God in demonstrating up front that we do not, and never will have, what it takes.

Jesus Christ is the only One capable of pleasing God. We simply cannot. I am fit only for death. Therefore, I will not only accept His death on the cross to deal with my past and future, I will also take up my own Cross and die, that He may live through me in the present. Then I, too, will be pleasing to God in every way: having no life of my own, but only His Life. This is Resurrection.

Taking Up The Cross Daily

> And [Jesus] said to all, "If anyone would come after me, let him deny himself and take up his cross daily and follow me." (Lk. 9:23)

We have stated before that the Cross is the means by which we enter, as well as live, the Christian life. Most Christians understand how we enter by way of the Cross. That is, we know that the death of Christ on the cross, the shedding of His blood, redeemed us from being dead in our sins. It satisfied the judgment of God against us and opened the door to fellowship with our heavenly Father.

This knowledge is sufficient for us to be saved, but if we only know the work of the Cross in terms of what Jesus did, we will be unable to live out the Christian life in a meaningful way. Though forgiven, we will find ourselves unable to forsake the sins we may have just repented of. Please note that Christ called upon people to take up *their* Cross, individually, and follow Him. Before He ever took up the physical cross and died for our sins, He told us to bear a Cross of our own as a prerequisite for following Him. Moreover, He tells us the Cross we are called to bear is not a once-and-for-all transaction. Jesus died for our sins once, and there is no further sacrifice to be made. God does not require Him to take up the Cross and die daily for our sins, yet He tells us to take up our Cross daily and follow Him. What is this?

Our passage in Luke gives us a clue that the passage in Matthew does not give. We have focused on taking up the Cross first, and then following Jesus. Now let us discuss the prelude to taking up the Cross: "Let him deny himself." The physical cross is nothing in and of itself. The Roman procurator who sentenced Jesus to death, Pontius Pilate, was alone responsible for the death of thousands of criminals on wooden crosses. If someone understands us to say that there is intrinsic power in a wooden upright post and crossbeam, then they miss the point.

The Cross is a spiritual principle, a philosophy, a standard, a symbol of self-denial. When we speak of

Christ's death on the physical cross we do not capitalize the word "cross." It is merely an instrument of death and it was a once-and-for-all event, thank God. But when we speak of the Cross as a call to self-denial and discipleship, we capitalize the word "Cross" because it is something more than a method of execution; it is an attitude of daily denying your Self, submitting your life into the Hands of Another, and giving ourselves up to die to our own will that we may follow His will.

But there is more. Please understand that the Cross is more than death; it is resurrection as well. This is unique to the Cross that we are called to bear. The physical cross always ended in death for its victims, Jesus Christ being the only exception. Similarly, the Cross as a principle working within us comprises death and life, burial and resurrection. God does not kill us in order to eradicate us or to render us non-existent. No, no, no, a thousand times no! All that is nailed to the Cross is one day brought to Resurrection! Did not Jesus say that if we lose our life we will save it? Did not Jesus say that if a grain of wheat falls to the earth and dies it brings forth an abundance of fruit? Hallelujah! This is the glory of the Cross! It is no glory to just die like a dog and cease to exist. No, we have something more glorious in mind than this. The Cross is not the end of me, but the beginning of me – a new man, a reborn me, a newly created me! Yet it is not I, but Christ! I cannot truly live for God until I truly die to myself. Then, the life I receive is resurrected life. Friends, when we overcome death and are resurrected, we cannot die again! Death has no more power over us! Therefore we must deny ourselves, take up the Cross *daily*, and follow Jesus.

Suppose a doctor asks, "Are you alive?" How would you respond? The question of life and death is applicable to your current state, not your previous experience. In other words, you would not say you are alive because you were born thirty years ago, or because you had a birthday last week. These are but historical facts; it does not necessarily mean you are alive and well *today*. Upon hearing of the death of someone, you might comment that they appeared to be quite well the day before. Nevertheless, they are dead today. Life is a daily condition, not a historical one.

In like manner, the question of spiritual Life is a matter of my condition today, not five, ten, twenty, or fifty years ago. Since this is the case, it is not enough to take up the Cross in the beginning. In order to live today, we must have His Life today; and in order to experience His Life daily, we must have His Death daily.

After many years we can perhaps smile, sing, appear loving, and be very engaged in spiritual work, yet have little Life, vitality, or freshness of spirit. All we have to do is open our mouth and people with discernment will quickly perceive if we are bringing forth Life or Death. We can repeat word for word what we said last week, but if we have not touched Life today, then we are only babbling spiritual phraseology. Or, we may hear a message and touch the Life of the Lord in the brother or sister who shares it. Then we bring it home and relate it to our brothers and sisters, employing the same words and illustrations, yet it fails to bring Life to the hearers. Why? It was a borrowed Life, not an actual entering into Christ and receiving from Him. The words may be correct, but without Life, even correct words are of little value.

Christ compared His flesh to the bread from heaven, called manna, which fell daily and sustained the Hebrews during their exodus from Egypt and subsequent wandering in the desert. Each day a new journey was made to collect fresh manna. All that was not eaten by sunset would become worms by sunrise. We are grateful for the multitudes who have tasted of the Lord's goodness, but the issue is not in tasting the Lord, but in feeding upon Him daily. Is this your experience?

Our Lord was born in a town called *Beth-Lehem*, which means, "House of Bread." Christ taught us to pray, "Give us this day our daily bread." Day by day we eat His flesh and drink His blood. This speaks of Life and daily communion. No matter what our previous history and walk with God, everything hinges upon today and now. Union must be maintained; fellowship must be unbroken; communion must be continuous; abiding is always a present action.

How do we maintain the Life of the Lord in us? What is the testimony of the apostle Paul? "But we have this treasure in jars of clay, to show that the surpassing power belongs to God and not to us. We are afflicted in every way, but not crushed; perplexed, but not driven to despair; persecuted, but not forsaken; struck down, but not destroyed; always carrying in the body the death of Jesus, so that the life of Jesus may also be manifested in our bodies. For we who live are always being given over to death for Jesus' sake, so that the life of Jesus also may be manifested in our mortal flesh. So death is at work in us, but life in you" (2 Cor. 4:7-12). In another place, he says, "I die daily" (1 Cor. 15:31). This is what it means to take up the Cross daily. We desire the Lord's Life daily, so we must have His Death working in us daily. There is no resurrection without crucifixion.

The answer to why there is so little power and genuine spiritual fruit in the lives of those who follow Jesus is a simple one: they desire the Life of the Lord, but not His Death. They want a daily pouring out of the Lord's Life, but they shun the prospect of daily sharing in His Death.

Why do we commit to teaching this in depth? Why do we belabor the point incessantly? Because the saints of the Lord are well instructed in living victoriously, being blessed, walking in power, overcoming the enemy, and living up to their potential. By comparison, the majority of them know next to nothing about self-denial, bearing their Cross, boasting in their weaknesses, being joyful in trials, winning by losing, gaining by giving up, working by resting, accepting both the bitter and the sweet as gifts from God, enduring hardness and accepting suffering. God desires to increase Christ and enlarge Christ in us; He therefore calls us to go back to the Cross and start over again.

Christ says we must die in order to live; we must first take up the Cross before we are fit to follow Jesus. This is the call of the Cross. Who will accept it?

"The greatest negative in the universe is the Cross, for with it God wiped out everything that was not of Himself: the greatest positive in the universe is the resurrection, for through it God brought into being all."

~ Watchman Nee

Chapter Three

The Hidden Wisdom

"We impart a secret and hidden wisdom of God, which God decreed before the ages for our glory." (1 Corinthians 2:7a)

Stress, depression, frustration, and confusion are usually the result of unmet expectations. That is, we expect things to be a certain way. We have an idea as to how we think things should go; but where did this idea come from? If things go differently than what we expect, then we are apt to become frustrated, angry, or upset. The greater the disparity between what we expect and what actually happens, the greater our discomfort. This shows that the difficulty is not in what we are experiencing, but in what we expect to experience.

The Lord Jesus is the most misunderstood Person of all. Millions of people expect something that He is not willing to provide, yet He offers every one of them something that they do not expect – or even want. This seems to be the Lord's way. A quick reading of the Gospels reveals just how little people understood Him. Even His own disciples had a hard time understanding Jesus. He would have shared much more with them, but they could not bear it (cf. Jn. 16:12). It is as though they were walking around in a fog. He is no more understood now than He was then. Jesus never acts or speaks in an expected way. That is why He is misunderstood, and often rejected.

Even though we have the benefit of a written record of His earthly life, the acts of the early Church, the letters of the apostles, and all the Old Testament history, prophecies, and teachings to help us know Him, Jesus remains a mystery. We are still walking around in a fog. How do I know? Because so many sincere believers are frustrated, angry, upset, confused, or depressed in their walk with the Lord. They do not understand what God is doing in their lives. And no one seems to be able to help them.

Paul explains it as "the hidden wisdom." What is wisdom? By itself, wisdom is the ability to see everything from God's perspective, for "the Lord sees not as man sees; for man looks at the outward appearance, but the Lord looks on the heart" (1 Sam. 16:7b). We cannot understand from our viewpoint. We must leave our earthly, natural, human ground and come up with Christ into the heavenlies so we may see as He sees (cf. Eph. 2:6).

So what does it mean when Paul says this wisdom is hidden? It means that this wisdom is not obvious. It is not readily seen. It is camouflaged in such a way that you can be looking right at it and yet not know it. This is why everyone looks and listens but so few people "get it." We can see it, and we can know it, but we must seek it out, because it hides from us.

Are we saying that we cannot know the Lord? No, but we are saying that we cannot know the Lord as long as we cling to our earthly perspective. There is a wisdom that comes from above, and there is a wisdom that is earthly (cf. Jam. 3:15-17). According to Scripture, these two are mutually exclusive. We cannot refer to both because they are contradictory.

A most remarkable example of the hidden wisdom is found in Luke 10:21: "He rejoiced in the Holy Spirit and said, 'I thank you, Father, Lord of heaven and earth, that you have hidden these things from the wise and understanding and revealed them to little children; yes, Father, for such was your gracious will.'" Jesus used parables when speaking to the multitude, but He explained everything to His disciples (cf. Mk. 4:34). Yet so often "they did not understand this saying... and it was concealed from them..." (Lk. 9:45ff).

The hidden wisdom is indeed revealed, but not to those who are wise in their own eyes. It is not gained through study, contemplation, or mental gymnastics. It is the revelation of the Father. The Father Who reveals Himself to little children is also the Father Who hides from the wise. Every child of God should know something of this hidden wisdom. If we do not know, then we should ask our Father to reveal it to us as His children. It is His nature to do so.

"Oh, what a wonderful God we have! How great are his riches and wisdom and knowledge! How impossible it is for us to understand his decisions and his methods!" (Rom. 11:33, NLT). This prevents us from becoming too dogmatic and sure of ourselves. At some point we just have to throw up our hands and say, "It's beyond me!" If we can figure out the Lord Jesus then we have made Him too small. To know Him is to know how little of Him we know. As the Lord continually reveals Himself, we find a depth and a breadth and a height that we could not have imagined. The hidden wisdom teaches us to see things from the perspective of the Heavenly Man.

So without further delay, let us look at some of the most prominent examples of hidden wisdom.

Life Out of Death

> "Whoever does not take his cross and follow me is not worthy of me. Whoever finds his life will lose it, and whoever loses his life for my sake will find it." (Mt. 10:38,39).

This is perhaps the foundation of the Hidden Wisdom. To our way of thinking, we ought to preserve and protect our life. Of course this is true to some extent. The Lord does not intend for us to be suicidal or foolish. What He has in mind here is something more than our physical existence.

"My life" is "me" or, as we commonly call it: Self. We do not truly appreciate how strong Self is. Self-reliance, self-assurance, self-confidence – all of these will rise up to resist the Lord until we lose our life by taking up the Cross daily (cf. Lk. 9:23). When the Cross has done its work then self-reliance becomes trust in the Lord, self-assurance becomes faith in the Lord, and self confidence becomes hope in the Lord. And that is only the beginning. The object is "not I, but Christ" (Gal. 2:20ff).

So the Hidden Wisdom teaches that in order to gain anything, we must give up everything. If we try to gain first, we lose. In the heavenly economy, Self plus Anything equals Nothing. But Christ plus Nothing equals Everything.

How many Christians are trying to add something to their spiritual walk: more love, more power, fresh anointing, gifts, prophetic words, etc.? But they have never lost their life. They have never taken up the Cross. And so, anything they think they get only increases Self and decreases Christ, and what looks like an outward gain is really a spiritual loss.

"He must increase, but I must decrease" (Jn. 3:30). This is the way to fullness, though it is contrary to all that we think. Indeed, I would say that most of our frustration comes from our simple unwillingness to embrace this decreasing. That is why after five, ten, or twenty years of God's dealings some people are just as unbroken as ever.

Before he was martyred, Jim Elliot wrote, "He is no fool who gives what he cannot keep to gain what he cannot lose." Meditate on that. It is better to embrace this sooner rather than later.

Wisdom Through Foolishness

> If any man among you seems to be wise in this world, let him become a fool, that he may be wise.

> For the wisdom of this world is foolishness with God. (1 Cor. 3:18,19)

Man places a high value on education, instruction, learning, and knowledge. Perhaps these things have their place, but in spiritual matters they mean nothing. Indeed, when the Spirit of the Lord begins to give us the Hidden Wisdom, we find it is contrary to the wisdom of this world. In order to see as He sees, we must be willing to embrace the unknown and the unfamiliar.

Paul warns that in the last days perilous times will come. He tells us of a sort of people who are "always learning, and never able to come to the full-knowledge (epignosis) of Truth" (2 Tim. 3:7). There is no lack of instruction and learning, no lack of Bible teachers and Bible studies, but there is a lack of experiential Truth. That is, people have truth as a "thing" instead of Truth as a Man. This demonstrates that an accumulation of knowledge does not guarantee an apprehension of Truth. The Bereans and the Pharisees both searched the Scriptures, but the Pharisees had a doctrine while the Bereans had a Man (compare Acts 17:10-12 with John 5:38-40). The difference is incalculable.

"God chose what is foolish in the world to shame the wise." (1 Cor. 1:27a). The word "shame" here means "disgrace." The Lord intends to disgrace and humiliate the wisdom of this world. How will He do it? By choosing what appears to be foolish. He will confound your own wisdom by letting you think you have everything figured out, only then to do something you do not expect. In the end, we must throw up our hands and say, "Lord, what do we know? Reveal Yourself to us!"

This is why Paul is not ashamed to admit that "not many of you were wise according to worldly standards" and yet are called (cf. 1 Cor. 1:26a). While some see this as a disadvantage, Paul sees it as an advantage. In fact, heavenly wisdom is so important that Paul tells us to become fools so that we may receive it. He considers his extensive training and religious education to be "dung" so that he may "gain Christ" (cf. Phil. 3). Naturally, those who are full of Self are too proud to look foolish, and they will reject this advice. But it is the way of the Hidden Wisdom.

Made Stronger Through Weakness

> But he said to me, "My grace is sufficient for you, for my power is made perfect in weakness." Therefore I will boast all the more gladly of my weaknesses, so that the power of Christ may rest upon me. For the sake of Christ, then, I am content with weaknesses, insults, hardships, persecutions, and calamities. For when I am weak, then I am strong. (2 Cor. 12:9-10)

Here is another tenet of the Hidden Wisdom – Strength from Weakness. Most Christians see weakness as weakness. They spend most of their time praying, or requesting prayer, for their circumstances to change. Paul used to pray that way, but no more: now he sees weakness as strength. Of course, this offends the natural man, but Paul explains it quite simply.

Three times the apostle asked the Lord to take away his "thorn in the flesh." It is pointless to debate what the "thorn" was, and for the purposes of our study it is irrelevant. Whatever you believe the thorn to be, it represented a weakness; something the gifted apostle despised, something he wanted to get rid of. He attacked the situation with prayer. Three times he asked the Lord to remove it from him, but the Lord did not do as Paul asked. Instead He said, "My Grace is sufficient, and My Power is perfected in your weakness."

Now Paul goes to the opposite extreme and rejoices in the things that make him weak. This is Hidden Wisdom indeed, and I doubt that one out of a million Christians really follow Paul's example here. Instead, most of us become angry, agitated, frustrated, sullen, downtrodden, and despondent when we encounter these "thorns." But that is why Paul was an apostle and we are not. Here is the secret: when I finally realize that I am too weak to do anything, the power of the Lord does in me and through me what I cannot do myself. The Cross intends to keep you in a state of weakness so that Christ must do everything for you. Thus, Paul says that "I can do all things through Christ Who strengthens me" (Phil. 4:13). This, in spite of the fact that his "thorn" remains!

Now it does not say that Paul made himself weak on purpose. We do not have to seek weaknesses, infirmities, tribulations, temptations, or trials. We already have them. The key is: how do we respond to them? We can fight them, or we can embrace them. Paul clearly shows us that it is not always God's will for us to be saved from the fire. Often we are called to walk through the fire, with no assurance except that His Grace is sufficient. In the fire we learn that "Grace" is a Man, just like Victory is a Man. To be delivered from weakness is one thing, but to meet Grace in my weakness is something else entirely.

Becoming the Greatest by Becoming the Least

> Whoever would be first among you must be slave of all... For everyone who exalts himself will be humbled, and he who humbles himself will be exalted. (Mk. 10:44; Lk. 14:11)

So far we have seen the Hidden Wisdom expressed in Life out of death, Wisdom out of foolishness, and Strength out of weakness. Here again the Lord strikes another blow to Self. According to our way of thinking, we ought to do everything possible to push ourselves to the front, rise to the top, and make a name for ourselves. But Jesus insists on humiliating the proud and giving grace to the humble.

A well-known musician was invited to a church to minister to them in song. He arrived on the appointed day, but when the time came for him to perform he could not be found. After some searching he was located in the church kitchen, washing dishes. The others were shocked, and asked why he was not on the platform. This brother simply replied, "There is no competition for the lowest place."

When we think of a king, we usually think of some human authority exerting their will upon their subjects with a haughty air. Regardless of whether the "king" calls himself pastor, priest, pope, prophet, or presbyter, all too often this is how we meet human authority. You can be sure that this authority does not represent the Lord Jesus, nor the Temple that He is building, regardless of what it calls itself, for it is not congruent with the Lord Himself. True authority is not found in title or position. Jesus, the King of Kings, shows us that true authority is serving, not lording over. In fact, Psalm 72 tells us what a true king is – someone who serves the people, provides for the poor, and defends those who cannot defend themselves.

We are being prepared for a kingdom. But our preparation is not in learning how to wear a crown or how to walk around with a glorious robe and scepter. One brother sings, "He's brought me low / so I could know / the way to reach the heights." In God's Kingdom, in order to go higher, we must go lower. That is the Hidden Wisdom.

Wealth and Prosperity by Becoming Poor

> ...As poor, yet making many rich; as having nothing, yet possessing everything. (2 Cor. 6:10)

How can a poor man make many people rich? The natural mind cannot understand it. But through the

Hidden Wisdom we learn that the true measure of wealth is not in the abundance of material possessions (Lk. 12:15). To outward appearances, Paul, who has "suffered the loss of all things" is a failure. The truth is that having gained Christ, he possessed all things in Him.

To the members of His Body in Smyrna, Jesus said, "I know your poverty: yet you are rich." To the believers in Laodicea, Jesus said, "You say, 'I am rich, I have prospered, and I need nothing', not realizing that you are wretched, pitiable, poor, blind, and naked" (compare Revelation 2:9 with 3:17). The ones who had nothing were rich, and the ones who had everything were poor. Which would you rather be associated with: Smyrna, or Laodicea? Sadly, many Christians equate blessing with material prosperity. They judge the success of their church or their ministry by numbers and dollar signs. Is this not the Laodicean spirit?

But when we look at Smyrna we see two themes: tribulation and resurrection. Again, it is the principle of Life out of death. Outwardly, Smyrna cannot match the boasting of Laodicea. But they take their name from "myrrh" – the anointing oil. Thus we see that the oil of gladness is poured out in difficult trials, and not in easy times. Smyrna represents the sweet-smelling incense produced through tribulation. Laodicea had no tribulation – but they had no perfume, either. I have often said that everyone wants apostolic revelation but no one wants apostolic persecution. Yet you cannot have one without the other.

"Blessed are the poor in spirit, for the Kingdom of God belongs to them" (Mt. 5:3). "Poor in spirit" here means spiritual bankruptcy. In Christ's Kingdom we gain by losing. When we are emptied, then we are filled. It is not a matter of how much money you have, but rather, how much of you does your money have? The nations pursue the "many things" and are deeply concerned about them (cf. Mt. 6:32). But only one thing is needed (Lk. 10:42a). Don't diversify; simplify. When we leave the ways of the world then Christ becomes our inheritance, our All in All, and we possess Treasure in Heaven, a Kingdom that will never end.

The Hidden Wisdom Revealed Through Death and Resurrection

> "Oh, what a wonderful God we have! How great are his riches and wisdom and knowledge! How impossible it is for us to understand his decisions and his methods!" (Rom. 11:33, NLT)

We have only scratched the surface of the Hidden Wisdom, but by now we have a good foundation to build upon. We are told that to save our life we must give up our life. To become wise we must become fools. To become strong we must become weak. To be exalted we must be humbled. To be rich we must become poor. But why is this?

We should see that the negatives (death, foolishness, weakness, humility, and poverty) are only the means through which the positives (life, wisdom, strength, exaltation, and true wealth) find expression. To put it another way, God's Purpose does not end with death, but with Life out of death. He does not stop with foolishness, but with Wisdom from foolishness. He does not cease working at the point of weakness, but carries through until He perfects strength from weakness. He will not rest with making you low, but intends to make you low so that He can bring you higher. He does not delight in poverty for poverty's sake, but makes you poor in order to make you rich.

Viewed from this perspective, all the negative things we may experience in this life are, in comparison, "light afflictions" which are "but for a moment." These so-called "light afflictions" (which can be so overwhelming at times) are actually working something glorious in us which is "beyond all comparison" (see 2 Cor. 4:17).

Jesus endured the Cross (the negative) because of the joy that was set before Him (Heb. 12:2). Apart from Resurrection, the Cross is dark, empty, confusing, and meaningless. It certainly looks like defeat. We may not even comprehend or see God's End in our brief life on earth. But with Resurrection everything becomes clear —looking back on it, we can see God's End was not Good Friday, but Resurrection Sunday. Resurrection always follows Crucifixion. In the end, God is justified. In the end, we will understand.

But for now, oh Lord, Your ways are past finding out! Lead us in Your narrow way. Teach us to embrace the Hidden Wisdom, which is Christ. Let us see into the heavenlies. Whether we live, or whether we die, we belong to You. Bless the Lord, O my soul, and all that is within me, bless His Holy Name! Amen.

"All God's plans have the mark of the cross on them, and all His plans have death to self in them."

~ E. M Bounds

Chapter Four

No Good Thing

"I know that nothing good dwells in me, that is, in my flesh."
(Romans 7:18a)

It is a great day for the Lord when a disciple of Jesus learns this most basic lesson: that in me, in my Self, in my flesh, dwells no good thing. This is a very difficult thing for people to learn. Jesus says that without Him we can do nothing. This verse is very well-known. Even so, Christians still attempt to do many things apart from the Lord. We feel like we simply must do something; anything. And even though the Bible says there is nothing good in our flesh, and the flesh is of no benefit, we spend a lot of time doing fleshly things apart from the Spirit of Jesus, thinking they are good and profitable. It is impossible to say for sure just how many of the things we "feel led" to do and say are actually just things we feel like doing and saying. A lot of the time the Lord has very little to do with it.

This problem is part of our Adamic nature and it is at work in us long before we are born-again. Before a person becomes a Christian they sometimes believe that they are intrinsically good or moral. At least, they say, there are not as bad as others. But those who know God know that in order for a person to enter the

Kingdom they must first see that their righteousness is as filthy rags, that all have fallen short of the glory of God, and that none are righteous in His sight. We protest that we are not so bad, but God says that the imagination of man's heart is only towards evil from his youth (cf. Gen. 8:21). To be saved, a person must stop claiming any righteousness of their own and accept God's verdict of them. No matter how good they may think they are compared to the rest of mankind, they are, nevertheless, sinners in need of a Savior. They cannot be born-again until and unless they recognize and acknowledge what the Lord says about them and their condition.

We who have received the Lord as Savior have come to this knowledge of ourselves at least once in our lives. There came a day when we despaired of saving ourselves, and instead of clinging to our righteousness, we confessed our sins and admitted our need for a Savior. At that moment, Christ accepted us as His disciples. Confessing our sinfulness did not hinder us from entering the Kingdom; on the contrary, it opened the door for us to go in. The self-righteous, on the other hand, are disqualified by their own good works. How differently the Lord judges things.

Knowing Christ, Knowing Self

When we are new disciples we have truly entered the Narrow Gate but there is still much we do not know and there is still much we need to learn. We know very little about Jesus, and we know very little about ourselves. And so, the Lord begins to lead us along the Narrow Path. He primarily wants to show us two things: who we are, and Who He is. These go hand-in-hand. Self-knowledge is just as important as Christ-knowledge. The revelation of Christ begins when God opens our eyes to see and know Jesus. The revelation of Self begins when God opens our eyes to see and know ourselves.

When we see the insufficiency of Self and the sufficiency of Christ, we will naturally despair of ourselves and look away to Jesus. On the other hand, if we do not see ourselves correctly, we will invariably imagine ourselves to be quite a bit better than we really are. We will mistake fleshly strength for spiritual strength and fleshly wisdom for spiritual wisdom. We will confess with our mouth that we cannot do anything apart from Jesus, but in actual practice we will take it upon ourselves to perform many works. In time all of these works become nothing. We will fail hundreds or thousands of times until we learn this lesson: if it comes from me, if it comes from my flesh, it is no good.

Before he saw the Lord, Paul was self-confident and dangerous. Those who trust in themselves have neither seen themselves nor seen the Lord. I am afraid that many people have the idea that Jesus came only to lend them a hand and help them feel more successful and fulfilled. Today the most popular Christian books tell us how to have a better life, how to prosper, how to be a "winner", how to improve our circumstances, and how to think nice, positive, encouraging thoughts about ourselves. The focus appears to be on making life here on earth more enjoyable and making believers more self-reliant and self-confident. This may not be the stated intention, but it is the inevitable result – and if a few Scriptures can be used to seemingly support the cause, so much the better.

It would be a mistake to equate holiness with misery and drudgery; but it is an even greater mistake to tell someone how wonderful they are unless they have first despaired of themselves and learned the lesson that Paul learned: "In me (that is, in my flesh) dwells no good thing."

Positive thinking is appropriate so long as I am living according to the Truth, but if I am unsurrendered to Jesus and living life according to my terms, then I am in no position to think about myself in a positive light: I am positively deceived. We do not need Self-Esteem, we need Christ-Esteem. The more we see of Jesus the less we will trust in ourselves. That is why, once Paul learned his lesson, he wrote, "We have no confidence in the flesh" (Phil. 3:3b). He then goes on to list quite a number of things that seem important in terms of religion – status, social order, education, and good works – all the things that tend to make you self-confident and self-righteous. With one grand stroke, Paul says, "Yet, I count them all as dung, that I may win Christ." (cf. Phil. 3:8). He simply discards what some people spend a lifetime trying to achieve. Here is a man who knows the sufficiency of God as well as the insufficiency of himself.

"That is fine for new believers," someone will say, "But I have been a Christian for many years now. I have a good relationship with God, I have had many spiritual experiences and have made great progress. This message is good for younger, less mature believers, but it does not apply to me." On the contrary, to lose all confidence in yourself is the mark of spiritual maturity. Real spiritual growth is evidence by increased confidence in Christ and a decreased confidence in myself. "He must increase, but I must decrease" (Jn. 3:30). You never outgrow these spiritual laws. Anyone who thinks they do not need to hear it again, did not really hear it the first time.

The Example of Joseph

We have a fine example of this in the life of Joseph. When Joseph was younger he realized that God had appointed him for a special purpose. God confirmed this special calling by giving Joseph prophetic dreams about his future. Joseph should have treasured these things in his heart and quietly waited for God to bring about His Will. But, being young and full of self-confidence, Joseph could not resist sharing these dreams with his father and brothers. As a result, his brothers became jealous and almost killed him. Joseph was sold into slavery and spent many years in prison. It appeared as though his dreams would not come true. Yet God was using all these circumstances to teach Joseph to have no confidence in the flesh.

After many seasons of God's dealings, Joseph was brought to the palace to interpret Pharaoh's dream. Here was an opportunity for Joseph to finally lift himself out of a terrible situation. Someone had finally recognized him for his gift and they had the power to reward him handsomely for it. But the younger, self-confident Joseph is now gone. He has finally learned the basic lesson of "not I, but Christ." "Can you interpret my dream?" Pharaoh asked. "It is not in *me*," Joseph replied, "But *God* will give you an answer" (cf. Gen. 41:16). And so He did, because now Joseph, emptied of himself, could be trusted. Joseph demonstrated even more wisdom and maturity in dealing with his brothers, freely demonstrating supernatural grace and love towards the ones who had intended evil towards him.

All of our circumstances, tests, and trials are designed to get us to the place where we can say along with Joseph, "It is not in me." God permits many things to come our way that we could otherwise avoid if we were not so cocky and self-confident. God has to work long and hard to get through to us, but what a wonderful day it is when we finally learn the lesson, bow our head, and surrender everything over to Him. Then He can really use us; but even if He does not use us, we are His nonetheless. Submitted to Him, we are equally content to be where He has placed us; whether we are sitting in the dungeon or sitting on the throne.

The Example of Peter

Peter is another good example of how every true disciple eventually learns that there is nothing good in his flesh. Peter began his walk with Jesus just as we did, acknowledging his sinfulness by saying, "Depart from me Lord, for I am a sinful man." Some will protest their own righteousness and feel as though they are doing God a huge favor by becoming a Christian. But Peter made a splendid beginning by frankly acknowledging himself as a sinner, and so the Lord took him just as he was and began to disciple him.

After making some progress, however, Peter started to lose touch with himself. He had followed Jesus for three years and enjoyed close fellowship with Him. He had both seen and performed miracles in Jesus' Name. To all outward appearances he was no longer a "sinful man", he was a "spiritual man." Before, Peter had considered himself unworthy to be in the presence of Jesus. In just a short period of time you find this "spiritual man" arguing along with the other disciples about which one of them will be the greatest! This ought to show us that there is a deeper death for us to die, and the more "spiritual" we become, the more easily we are deceived by our own spirituality.

If a dentist offers to remove one of your good teeth you will probably refuse. But if that tooth develops a cavity, it is only a matter of time before you seek out the dentist and have it removed. The greater the pain, the quicker you seek relief. Similarly, when the Lord first speaks of taking up the Cross, we are apt to respond as Peter did: "Not so, Lord! This will never happen to You – or me!" We see no need for death because Self has not yet become painful enough to us. When we are tired of the pain that comes from living in the flesh, then we will gladly ask God to decrease us so that He can be increased. Until then, no amount of teaching, argument, or doctrine is enough to convince a person.

Peter held out until the very end. He was a very difficult case, but the Lord was patient. When Jesus said that all would forsake Him, Peter protested and announced that even if all the other disciples fled, he would never leave Jesus. Outwardly he acted and spoke as a deeply committed believer and disciple. But when temptation came, he could not even stay awake long enough to pray. Perhaps he did not feel prayer was necessary; he was strong enough to resist without praying! Then, when Jesus allowed Himself to be arrested, Peter tried to defend Him with a sword. All of these examples demonstrate how very little Peter knew about himself.

It was not until Peter actually did deny the Lord three times that he came to learn the same lesson that Paul learned: "I know that in me (that is, in my flesh) dwells no good thing." After he denied the Lord he went out and wept bitterly. Finally he was broken. He hated himself for what he had done. If he was capable of denying the Lord Jesus then he was capable of anything. At last he had seen something of himself, and he was ashamed.

Strangely enough, the more unworthy Peter believed himself to be, the more the Lord sought to restore and encourage him! The Lord does not break the bruised reed. When Peter was strong and arrogant, the Lord weakened him with a rebuke. When Peter was sufficiently weak and humble, the Lord strengthened him with encouragement. What a glorious Lord we have, Who meets us exactly where we are and ministers to us accordingly!

Failure Serves God's Purpose

Jesus was not surprised or disappointed when Peter failed. In like manner, He is not surprised or disappointed when you fail. Rather, He is waiting for you to fail so that you will be reduced to Him. He has no illusions about you and He knows you through and through. He knows however much your spirit may be willing, your flesh is weak. Our weakness is not the trouble – the trouble is our unwillingness to acknowledge the weakness.

Paul had no confidence in the flesh, so he could say, "I will boast all the more gladly of my weaknesses, so that the power of Christ may rest upon me" (2 Cor. 12:9b). But we do not boast in our weakness the way Paul did. We either refuse to admit it, or we hide it, or we try to improve upon it, or we try to make up for it by over-compensating in some other area. People will fight and argue with me on this point because they desperately want to salvage something for themselves.

They have a fragile self-esteem and this kind of news is too painful to bear.

But I bring you good news, dear Christian friend! This failure of Self is the very key to living the Christian life. As painful as it is, the bitter tears of failure provide the water for nurturing the Precious Seed that is planted in your heart of hearts and will make it grow. To despair of ourselves is the very key that opens the door to all the power, the victory, and fruitfulness in Christ that we seek. "I know that in me (that is, in my flesh) dwells no good thing." I know it, Paul says. No good thing. I know that in me, in my flesh, in my Self, there is nothing. Apart from Him I am nothing. He is Everything. Christ in me is my only Hope. In one part of me, my flesh, dwells no good thing. In the other part of me, in my spirit, Christ lives.

Why do you lack power? Why are you unable to walk in continual victory? Why do you not see fruitfulness? Because power, victory, and fruitfulness only come to a person who is standing on resurrection ground. God's holy anointing oil was not to be poured out upon the flesh. God does not grant these things to people who are still living for themselves. Resurrection Life is for those who have died already – how could it be otherwise? Unless a man has passed through death he cannot know anything about resurrection. If a person will not consent to the Cross, then they will not die, and if they will not die then they cannot be resurrected. If they are not resurrected, they cannot ascend with Christ and be seated with Him in the heavenlies, for "flesh and blood cannot enter the Kingdom of God" (1 Cor. 15:50).

If you have a Bible Promise Book, one of your favorite promises is probably Philippians 4:13: "I can do all things through Christ Who strengthens me." Keep in mind, however, that the same man who said this also said, "I am crucified with Christ" (Gal. 2:20). I can do all things through Christ Who strengthens me, but this Strength is only perfected in my weakness (cf. 2 Cor. 12:9). Also remember that "Apart from Me, you can do nothing" is a golden promise as well, because I promise you that anything you do apart from Jesus will amount to nothing!

How to Enter In

Why is it so difficult for a rich man to enter the Kingdom of God? Because wealth creates the illusion of control and this breeds self-confidence. Money is like a drug that makes one feel invincible. Once the money is gone, the illusion is destroyed and there is a natural humility that follows.

Those who are rich in spiritual experiences find it equally difficult to enter in. Often when a person considers themselves to be "apostolic" or "prophetic" or "spiritual" or "called to the ministry" they present a formidable challenge. It is most difficult to teach them anything or even discuss something with them because they are not poor in spirit, they are rich in spirit. They like to argue, fuss, debate, and find fault with others.

Like the younger Joseph, they always have a dream, vision, or word to speak, but they lack wisdom and maturity. They are the type of people who will walk halfway around the world to preach a message, but will not drive across the street to listen to one. They want to be seen and heard, but they cannot bear to see or hear others.

Friends, it may be difficult to enter in, but it is not impossible. It is impossible with man, this is true; but with God, all things are possible. The quicker we accept man's impossibility, the quicker we can accept God's possibility. The way we enter in is right here: "I have been crucified with Christ. It is no longer I who live, but Christ who lives in me." (Gal. 2:20). God's solution to our problem is to nail us to the cross with Jesus. If we will accept this sentence of death then all our problems will die right along with us. The problems will not die until we are thoroughly dead ourselves. But the day we cease striving and meekly accept the Cross, we will find everything is settled. We can protest our innocence and die slowly like the two thieves, or we can quietly commit ourselves into God's hand and give up the ghost.

What shall we do to enter in? The first thing to do is to stop doing. Let us learn to breathe words along these lines: "Today, Lord, I give up. I am finished. I surrender. I know now that in my flesh dwells no good thing. Apart from You I am nothing, and apart from You I can do nothing. I do not even know how to pray. I accept the sentence of death, and I trust You to raise me from the dead. As I am decreased, may You be increased. I have learned that I cannot; therefore, I will not. Into Your hands I commit my spirit. You are the Resurrection and the Life, and I will wait for You to raise me from the dead. I will not raise myself. Let Your Strength be perfected in my weakness."

When this is a practical reality for a person, and not just a theory, it will sound like this: "I used to be quite confident in myself and very sure, but today I have no confidence in myself. I used to be very active, but today I am content to be still. If God should rise within me, I will certainly obey Him; but if He does not move, I dare not step out ahead of Him. I will work, but I will not work according to what I want to do. Instead, I will work according to His desire and Power that works in me, this power that strengthens me to do all things, this power that is perfected in my weakness. I no longer hide my weaknesses, I delight in them; for they allow me to know true Strength. I look for Christ in me to overcome my inability. I have surrendered myself over to Him as a bondservant, as a prisoner of the Lord. If I live, I am the Lord's. If I die, I am the Lord's. So, in both life and in death, I belong to Him."

Friends, Jesus did not say, "I am the Crucifixion and the Death." He said, "I am the Resurrection and the Life." Meditate upon the difference! Resurrection and Life is on the other side of this Cross that Jesus requires us to take up. The Cross is the Gate of Life that leads us into the Promised Land of Resurrection. Let us embrace the Cross and delight in the Cross, for it is the power of God for achieving His Purpose. Amen.

Measure thy life by loss
and not by gain,

Not by the wine drunk,
but by the wine poured forth,

For love's strength
standeth in love's sacrifice,

And he who suffers most
has most to give.

~ Lilias Trotter

Chapter Five

The Need for Brokenness

"The LORD is near to the brokenhearted and saves the crushed in spirit. Many are the afflictions of the righteous, but the LORD delivers him out of them all." (Psalm 34:18,19)

"The sacrifices of God are a broken spirit; a broken and contrite heart, O God, you will not despise." (Psalm 51:17)

The fundamental need of a disciple of Jesus Christ is not more power, but more brokenness. The majority of Christians today are not too unlike the original twelve disciples of the Lord. We observe the Twelve arguing over who is the greatest; asking to sit on His right hand and on His left; desiring to call down fire from heaven upon those who oppose them; refusing to wash each other's feet; protesting the need for the Lord to go to the cross, even drawing the sword to defend Him in the garden.

We see that the disciples were not endued with power from on high until they were of one mind and one accord, together in one place, after the crucifixion and resurrection of the Lord Jesus Christ. While it is true that they enjoyed a measure of spiritual power during the Lord's ministry on earth, we see how even this little taste of heavenly ability puffed them up. Jesus sent them forth and gave them authority over evil spirits. So it happened that when they returned, they exclaimed, "Lord! Even the demons are subject to us through Your name!" Even this small accomplishment made them rejoice and exalt in themselves. Jesus told them that this little bit of success was hardly worth rejoicing over. Later on, we find the disciples rebuking others who used the Name to cast out demons. Why? Because "they are not one of us." Patiently, Jesus tells them to stop forbidding the others, because "he that is not against us is for us." We see how quickly pride was able to gain a foothold.

What a tragedy it would have been to pour out the Holy Spirit in His fullness upon the disciples in such a condition! They were thoroughly unfit and unprepared to handle such power. Why? Not because they were insincere. No doubt they were very sincere. After all, they had given up everything and were following the Lord. Nevertheless, they were yet unbroken. That is to say, they were following the Lord and even had a taste of spiritual power, but they had not yet taken up the Cross. Over and over again Christ said they must take up the Cross, but they could not understand what He meant. They even sought to prevent the Lord from taking up His cross.

The disciples could not be entrusted with much power at this point because they were not sufficiently dead to themselves. The slightest accomplishment would only be grounds for foolish boasting and further arguments to see who was to be the greatest among them. Hence, they were told to stay in Jerusalem and wait until they would be invested with power from on high. As proud men they were found arguing on many occasions, but as broken men they were finally in one mind and one accord. Thus, the Spirit came, and with the Spirit, the fullness of power.

Today the call is for unity, but we need to see that unity cannot be achieved by calling people to unity. Unity is achieved when we each take up the Cross and die to our minute opinions and lay down our petty arguments and prejudices. Then, and only then, will we have to one mind. A broken spirit is a peaceful spirit, and is able to put up with others. Contentious, unbroken, hard, stubborn people can never be in one accord. The sacrifice God desires is a broken and contrite spirit.

More of the Lord and Less of Me

Indeed, as the Lord calls us back to the Cross to become disciples of Jesus, He intends to first humble us before empowering us. It is not a question of His supply, nor is His Life to be measured in terms of some, more, or plenty. Either the Life is present, or it is not present. The Lord's Life is a rich Life, and it fills the believer with *all* the fullness of God. We may say of a brother or a sister, that they "really know the Lord in a powerful way" or that they are "full of Life" or they have a "strong anointing." Of course we all have different gifts and abilities as the Spirit enables us. But we should not use phraseology which implies that some brothers and sisters have more of the Lord's Life than other brothers and sisters. We categorically reject this idea. God is no respecter of persons:

> [God] has blessed us with every spiritual blessing in heavenly places in Christ." (Eph. 1:3)

> For in [Christ] the whole fullness of deity dwells bodily, and you have been filled in him, who is the head of all rule and authority. (Col. 2:9,10)

> He who did not spare his own Son but gave him up for us all, how will he not also with him graciously give us all things? (Rom. 8:32)

What are these Scriptures telling us? That we are blessed with every spiritual blessing, filled with the fullness of God in Christ, and have received all things freely through Him. No single believer is any more "anointed" or powerful than any other.

Please tell me, saint of God, what it is that you lack spiritually; for these Scriptures demonstrate conclusively that you are already filled with all that God has and is. How much is all? How full is full? How complete is complete? If there is a lack in our lives, let us readily admit that the lack is not on the Lord's part, and it is not because we are inferior to other, more "powerful" believers. The question is not how to get more of the Lord, but how to release the Life which is already hidden within us, obscured behind the veil of our flesh. To put it another way, it is not more of the

The Need for Brokenness

Lord that we need, but less of ourselves. We must be broken.

Christians today are encouraged to seek more power, more anointing, and more gifts. I have stood before these precious believers and led them in the singing of choruses which cry, "More love, more power, more of You in my life." To be sure such a desire is good and sincere. The saints are so hungry for the presence of the Lord. I have watched thousands stream forward in hopes of obtaining some fresh outpouring of spiritual power or anointing. I have both led them in the pursuit of more power and joined them in the pursuit. Day and night I searched for spiritual power that I might overcome my sins, be a witness for the Lord, and have a powerful ministry which reached thousands.

But a day came when the Lord gave me a revelation of Christ in me, and I in Christ. That day was like walking out of one room, entering another, and closing the door behind me. From that day forward I realized that I was complete in Christ, filled with all that God has and all that He is. From that day forward I saw that the problem is not in obtaining more from the Lord, but in allowing Him to break me and humble me so that I may no longer hinder Him through my own foolishness, pride, natural wisdom, fleshly lusts, and divided heart. I needed to decrease, and He would increase in direct proportion to my decrease. If I decreased but a little, He would increase but a little. But with much decrease of me there would be much increase of Him. With less of me, there would be more of Him in my life!

The Pursuit of Power

I will state it again: most Christians eagerly, even greedily, seek the power of God, but they resist anything that would seek to decrease, humble, test, or prove them. They want the power, but they refuse the weakness. Stated differently, they relish the bright sunshine, gentle breeze, and singing birds, but they curse the dark night when the coyotes howl and the rain falls. When God performs as expected then all is well, but when He fails to perform as expected, the countenance grows dark and the soul is depressed.

And how many "Spirit-filled" believers have we met that seemed to carry about a certain power and seemed to be very spiritual while sitting in church, yet they could not control their tongue or keep a reign upon their critical spirit? Their power only gives them an occasion to glory in their flesh and compare themselves in a favorable light with others. Mark this well: any power that does not come by way of weakness will ruin people such as this.

We must never seek the power of Pentecost without first tasting the suffering of the Cross. The Cross is Power disguised in Weakness. There is a saying, "Absolute power corrupts absolutely." We can just as well say that spiritual power obtained apart from the weakness of the Cross will corrupt also. This is why the

Lord leads us first to Calvary, then on to Pentecost. We dare not bypass Calvary in our haste to experience Pentecost.

In spite of this spiritual truth, observe how little attention is paid to the necessity of brokenness among those who so eagerly speak of the power of God. We should be afraid of listening to anyone who teaches us about the power of God but does not teach us about the necessity of brokenness. Invariably the power, once received, will pollute the spirit and pride will set in. Weakness, humility, brokenness, suffering, pouring out our lives, taking up the Cross – this language seems to be lost among the seekers of power. How tragic that is!

The Seasons of the Spirit

Yes, the Lord in us is full of might and power; yet He will not intrude upon our will and overwhelm us. Sometimes we wish He would do so. But that is not His way. He desires for us to cooperate with His Spirit. When we come to Him and present ourselves as instruments to be used, He begins to mold us and shape us into suitable vessels. If we see this process as beginning and ending in a one-time act of consecration, or a single moment of surrender, or a solitary life-changing event, then we underestimate just how thorough and far-reaching this process will be. It spans many years and is marked with many mountains and valleys, gardens and deserts.

The one so committed may now expect to encounter many seasons of light and darkness, sunshine and rain, heat and cold, sweetness and bitterness. At the outset he may think he will be happy, light, and carefree now that he has tasted some of the Lord's power. He will rejoice for that season, and then the sun will set and the dark night of the soul will begin... All that was gained now seems to have been lost. The former sweetness is nowhere to be found. Everything is dreary and burdensome. When this season is accomplished, the sun rises again and the Christian rediscovers the joy of his salvation. The vows are renewed and the spirit begins to soar. Prayer and praise now pour forth like water. Everything is effortless and spontaneous.

But then, strangely enough, that season passes and the dark night sets in once again. Why is this? The Lord is teaching us to live apart from our circumstances. Eventually we will learn how to live above our environment and walk by faith, not by sight.

I remember times when I experienced the presence of God so powerfully that I thought surely I could not sin after such an experience. Remembering my many sins and failures, I surmised that was all behind me now that I had tasted of such a heavenly sphere. Failure seemed impossible. How happy I was that now I had met the Lord in a powerful way, or had some spiritual experience, or heard some special word from the Lord, for with this I was sure to be victorious from now on. How utterly distressing it was to find myself less than a week later wallowing in the same sin and defeat as before! Truly perplexed, I would struggle along until

Sunday, where I would go forward to receive the prayers of the saints. Once again I was lifted up into the throne room and felt as though I could reach out and touch the Lord. Surely I need not fail again! But of course, once I left the mountaintop and descended again into the valley, I found the old lusts ever present with me, ready to reclaim me as soon as I arrived back from my latest encounter with the Lord.

Perhaps this has been your experience as well. We must learn sooner rather than later that discipleship is a process of tearing down in order to build up. We cannot expect to have a single mountaintop experience with the Lord and then assume that from then on the work of the Cross is completed in us. When we are standing with the Lord in the New Jerusalem we may lay down our Cross. Until then, we dare not entertain the thought that we have already been made perfect. We must deny ourselves and take up the Cross daily.

So if there is a seeming difference in the "level" of anointing or power or spirituality among believers, it is definitely not because some have more of the Lord than others. Let this be an encouragement to you. Indeed, Christ is not divided, and of His fullness we all share. We are all baptized into the same Spirit. The difference is that some saints are more broken than others. Some have passed through many seasons of tearing down and building up, while some, after many years of experience, are still resisting the Lord and refusing to lay down their lives. Some have recognized God's dealings and have submitted to them, while others have misunderstood or been totally ignorant of God's dealings with them. The ones who have been sufficiently broken eventually manifest very little of their self, and very much of Christ. God must work long and hard with us to bring us to this place, but what a glorious day it is when we are able to bow our heads and finally surrender everything. What joy it is to look back over all that the Lord has led us through and realize His purpose in both the good times and the bad times, to see the goodness and the severity of God in His dealings with us.

Four Examples of Brokenness
Example One: The Bread of Life

The Cross represents the principle of brokenness in the disciple of the Lord Jesus. Let us look to the Scriptures for some examples of brokenness.

The night He was betrayed, we are told that the Lord Jesus "took bread, and when he had given thanks, he broke it and gave it to them, saying, This is my body, which is given for you. Do this in remembrance of me" (Lk. 22:19). Many times the Lord told the disciples and the crowds, "I am the Bread of Life." He commanded them to eat His flesh and drink His blood. This is one of my favorite passages of Scripture, and one which I refer to constantly when discussing this subject. Many turned aside and no longer followed the Lord after He said this. How can this Man give us His flesh to eat? Because He is the Bread of Life.

The Need for Brokenness

The little communion wafers given in churches today fail to adequately represent the Bread of Life. At the Passover there was one loaf, and it was broken into pieces so that all could eat a portion of it. Today the wafers come to us already divided and this fails to show us the vital truth that in order to partake of the Life, there must be a breaking. The churches are certainly divided today, so perhaps this is a good representation of their division! There is one Loaf, not many loaves. Jesus is the Bread which came down from heaven. How can we receive Him? He must be broken for us. After blessing the bread, and breaking it, He plainly tells us, "This is My body."

It is interesting to note here that the blessing Jesus prayed over the bread is the same blessing the Jews bless their bread with today. It has not changed in centuries. The Scriptures do not record it because it was written for the Jews, and they already knew it:

> "Blessed are You, O Lord our God, King of the Universe, Who brings forth bread from the earth."

After the blessing, Jesus broke the bread. The Passover ceremony also calls for a portion of the bread to be wrapped in a napkin and hidden, to be retrieved later. Through this the Lord is showing us His crucifixion and resurrection in the blessing, the breaking, the "burying" or hiding, and the "bringing forth again" of the bread. He is the Bread which has come down from heaven: broken, buried, and brought forth from the earth. The traditional communion wafer destroys this beautiful parable. Indeed, our Lord is one

Loaf which is broken, that we may all share in His Life. Hallelujah! This illustrates the need for brokenness so that Life may flow out.

Example Two: A Grain of Wheat

Again, for an example of brokenness, let us look to the Lord's words to us in His final hours on earth: "And Jesus answered them, "The hour has come for the Son of Man to be glorified. Truly, truly, I say to you, unless a grain of wheat falls into the earth and dies, it remains alone; but if it dies, it bears much fruit. Whoever loves his life loses it, and whoever hates his life in this world will keep it for eternal life" (Jn. 12:23-25).

How remarkable are the Lord's words here. He begins by saying that it is time for Him to be glorified. When we think of the Lord being glorified, we think of His baptism when the Spirit descended upon Him as a dove and the Voice of God declared Him to be His Son. Or we think of the mountain when His appearance became dazzling white and the brightness of His Glory was shown to Peter, James, and John. How strange then that Jesus talks of being glorified by a cruel death! It seems contrary to what we have been led to believe thus far. But the Lord explains why His death is necessary.

When the Lord Jesus humbled Himself and accepted the limitations of a human body, He was only able to be in one place at a time. For all the people that He did heal, there were many millions who remained sick. He simply could not, as a Man, be everywhere at once. He was limited by time and space. In one place He seemed frustrated with a holy frustration: "I came to cast fire on the earth, and would that it were already kindled! I have a baptism to be baptized with, and how great is my distress until it is accomplished!" (Lk. 12:49,50). See how the Lord is restrained, and seems to be aching to come forth. He is like the grain of wheat; a Seed surrounded by the outer shell of His physical body.

Pick up an acorn. What are you holding in your hand? A seed, yes. But what else? A tree? Yes, once the seed is buried it will one day produce a tree. But what else are you holding in your hand, besides a tree? A forest! Because, from that seed will come a tree, and from that tree will come many more seeds, and from those seeds will come many more trees, and so on. So what you hold in your hand is not a mere seed, but a forest.

Jesus says the Kingdom of God is "as if a man should scatter seed on the ground. He sleeps and rises night and day, and the seed sprouts and grows; he knows not how. The earth produces by itself, first the blade, then the ear, then the full grain in the ear." (Mk. 4:26-28). Dear friend, this is glorious! We don't have to do anything with the seed but cast it into the ground and forget about it! "The earth produces by itself." God will bring forth the fruit if we will bury the seed! Do you want to be fruitful? Humble yourself! Cast yourself into the ground and allow yourself to be broken so that the Seed and the Fruit may come forth.

Now, Jesus says if the seed will not fall to the earth and die, it will remain alone. Take the seed home and place it on your desk. Will it become a forest there? Of course not. Why not? That forest is inside the shell, but it cannot come forth on its own. You see, the potential is there, for there is life in the seed. But the inner life is entombed by an outer shell. How do we get that which lies dormant within the shell to come out of the shell? We must bury the seed in the ground – the seed must "die" and give up being a seed. The shell must be broken then that which is within the shell will come forth. When it dies, it brings forth "much fruit."

You see, the issue is not the ability of the Life to spring forth, but the brokenness of the vessel which holds the Life captive! It is not that we need more power, but that we need more brokenness. When we are properly broken we will find the indwelling Christ is more than sufficient.

Example Three: The Alabaster Box

> And while he was at Bethany in the house of Simon the leper, as he was reclining at the table, a woman came with an alabaster flask of ointment of pure nard, very costly, and she broke the flask and poured it over his head. (Mk. 14:3)

The ointment here represents Anointing, or Life. I use the terms synonymously. It was very precious, but it was contained within an alabaster box. Alabaster is a kind of stone used to make vases. But the same stone was also used to make caskets! Again, we have Life encased within Death. The inward release is contingent upon the outward breaking.

How many of us cherish the vessel more than the ointment? Friends, the vessel is nothing. Let us look beyond the vessels and instruments of the Lord and only note if the precious ointment is coming forth freely or is inhibited. The vessel houses the Life and must be broken. If we wish to be containers of this heavenly ointment, then let us ask the Lord to break us so that the hidden fragrance and anointing of Christ may come forth.

Example Four: The Veil of the Temple

> And the veil of the temple was torn in two, from top to bottom. (Mk. 15:38)

The veil of the Temple was a thick curtain which separated the Holy of Holies from the rest of the temple. What was special about the Holy of Holies? It was where the presence of God remained. No one could step into the presence, or even look behind the curtain, without falling over dead. Only the high priest could enter, and even then only once a year.

But when the Lord Jesus died on the cross, the thick curtain which stood as a barrier between the presence of God and the people was split down the middle from top to bottom. Why top to bottom? To demonstrate that it was God Himself who split the veil. Had the veil been torn from bottom to top, it could perhaps be explained away that man was responsible. To tear the veil from top to bottom is indeed a miracle. What does it signify? Of course it means that the death of Christ opened the way for us to approach the throne of grace without fear of death (Heb. 10:19,20). That is the obvious meaning. Yet we know also that the three sections of the temple – the Holy of Holies, the Holy Place, and the Outer Court – represent the spirit, soul, and body of man. The Holy of Holies is the spirit of man where Christ dwells. In between the inner man and the outer man stands a thick veil.

We stand by our assertion that each believer is complete and contains the entire fullness of God, but we also acknowledge that the veil of the flesh must be torn in two in order for that fullness to come forth. How often we meet a brother or a sister and we sense their preciousness, but there is something that prevents the Life from coming forth as it should. That "something" is the fleshly veil which remains intact. We can only hope that they will allow the Lord to tear and break them so that the Life can come forth. Similarly, when we sense a lack, we should not pray for more of the Lord, or seek more power, as though Christ living in us is not sufficient. Instead, we can ask the Lord to break us and tear away the veil that is keeping His Life from coming forth.

The Cross Accomplishes This Breaking

Now we have before us four examples from the Scriptures of what it means to be broken and why it is necessary: the bread, the grain of wheat, the alabaster box, and the temple veil. There is yet another point to be made from these four examples. In each instance, the Lord mentions His death and resurrection. The principle of the Cross is central to each illustration. The blessing and breaking of the bread speaks of His death and resurrection; the grain of wheat speaks of His being glorified through His substitutionary death; the alabaster box is connected to the Lord's anointing for burial (Mk. 14:8); and the temple veil is torn at the moment of His death on the cross. These are not mere coincidences.

The Lord has continually called us to deny ourselves, take up the Cross, and follow Him. We are not left to wonder what it means to take up the Cross, or what God hopes to accomplish in us when we do so. In these examples He is showing us what it means, and why it must be so. What is He saying? That we must be broken before we can bring forth Life; that to save our life we must give up our life, lay down on the altar, and offer ourselves as a living sacrifice to God. Only then may we truly live for God. Only then can we be vessels through which Life may flow.

One time the disciples asked the Lord, "Increase our faith" (Lk. 17:5). Do you remember how the Lord responded to this request? It is a very strange response. Today we ask the Lord to increase our faith, increase our patience, increase our love, increase our self-control; give us more. Strangely enough, it seems as though these repeated requests often go unanswered. We are still asking for "more" and it has been many years since we first asked. It is the same with the disciples. They asked the Lord to increase their faith. Instead of giving them more faith, He basically told them that they didn't need more faith, because they had enough already. How do you like that response?

Watchman Nee was once asked to help a sister who insisted that she needed more patience. She told him of all the times she lost her temper and how terribly she behaved. She prayed and prayed for patience, but to no avail. So she asked Watchman Nee if he would agree with her in prayer that God would give her patience so that she would no longer lose her temper. Our brother said, "This I cannot do." Stunned, she asked why not. "Because I can assure you that God will not answer your prayer," he answered. This sister became angry. "What do you mean God will not answer my prayer?" she demanded. "Am I so far gone that He will not hear me anymore?" "No, I do not mean exactly that," Nee explained, "What I mean is this: God will not give you more patience, because you have no need of patience." Now the woman was nearly beside herself with anger. "What do you mean I have no need of patience? I am always losing my temper and acting in a most regrettable manner. How can you say I do not need patience?" "Dear sister," he calmly replied, "it is not patience that you need; it is Christ."

He went on to explain that all we have need of is in Christ, and Christ is in us. Therefore, we do not need to seek God for a little patience here, a little faith there. Instead, we must see that we are complete in Christ, and ask God to humble us and break us, so that Christ will be my Patience, and that Christ will be my Faith, and that Christ will be my Righteousness, etc. We have every spiritual blessing already in Christ, but that Life is for the most part trapped within the alabaster box. We love the alabaster box more than the ointment, but we cannot have the ointment without breaking the container.

Dear friend, are you an intact and enclosed container, or a broken one? Is Christ bound up and restrained within your heart, or is your heart free and emancipated so that He may come forth through you? Have you expressed your willingness to die to yourself so that you may bring forth a lot of fruit, or are you like the seed which refuses to die and therefore remains alone? Has Christ's Life been released in you and through you, or does the veil need to be torn in two?

Oh, let us go back to the Cross and humble ourselves so that He may have freedom of expression through us! Do we desire the presence of the Lord? Then let us ask the Lord to decrease us through the Cross, for "the Lord is near to the brokenhearted and saves the crushed in spirit."

"The measure and the swiftness of our yielding will be the measure of the putting forth of His power."

~ Lilias Trotter

Chapter Six

The Secret of Spiritual Power

"God opposes the proud, but gives grace to the humble. Submit yourselves therefore to God. Resist the devil, and he will flee from you." (James 4:6b,7)

There is a principle at work in our life and walk with the Lord, and it is the principle of strength out of weakness. "The meek are blessed, for they will inherit the earth" (Mt. 5:5). If we want the blessing of the Lord then we must learn what it is to be meek, for the proud will not inherit anything from Him.

The way of the world says that in order to be stronger, we must build ourselves up and seek strength and dominance over others. Christians everywhere are keenly interested in how to be increased, how to be stronger, how to take authority, how to rise up, how to get more. They look for methods, formulas, and techniques for becoming bigger and better. The results have been disappointing. Many mistakes have been made and many people have been hurt and disillusioned.

The Lord has a different approach for us to take. He invites us to accept weakness in order to be strengthened. We do not become strong by embracing strength, but by embracing weakness! This is the secret of all spiritual power. When Paul learned this secret he was able to say, "When I am weak, then I am strong" (2 Cor. 12:10b). This makes no sense to the natural man. I do not remember ever hearing anyone begin a teaching on spiritual warfare with this verse. It is no wonder, then, that these teachings never seem to produce any lasting fruit.

This passage of Scripture from James gives us further insight into why the strong are weak, and why the weak are strong. Our study of this verse may be divided into four distinct sections. Let us look at each one individually.

God Resists the Proud

Christians are full of many plans, many pursuits, many thoughts, many words, many things. It is impossible to say just how much of the flesh is involved in the things we undertake in the Name of Jesus. We know that they cannot be purely spiritual works because often there is little spiritual fruit to be found. We labor and toil and work but it seems as if we make little or no progress. It seems as if something is always blocking our way and preventing us.

The automatic assumption is that anything which resists us or hinders us is of satanic origin. That is, if we encounter difficulty in our spiritual walk, our first reaction is to rebuke the devil, or ask the saints to pray for us to have a clear way. Certainly the devil will attempt to hinder us from anything we undertake that glorifies God and threatens the darkness. Yet we learn from James 4:6 that there is Someone Else who can resist us. There is Another Who carefully watches what we do, and frequently hinders us from making progress.

It comes as a shock and surprise to some Christians to see one day that God, not the devil, is resisting them. The Lord Himself resists us, closes doors, causes things to be unfruitful, and spoils all our plans. How so? Because "God opposes the proud." This resistance from God is insurmountable. It is a fearful thing to fight the Lord. We spend most of our lives wrestling with God instead of cooperating with God, and in the end we have nothing to show for it. So much time and effort is wasted because we proceed in our own, stubborn way. We attribute all difficulties to the devil, or other people, or our circumstances, or our environment, and fail to recognize that the Lord Himself is resisting us.

God resists the proud. This is an active resistance that will block our path like a huge rock or a great chasm. All who walk in pride are in league with the devil himself, and will receive the same judgment (cf. 1 Tim. 3:6). Brothers and sisters, this is a serious matter. If we harbor the least bit of pride then we will find ourselves on the wrong side of the Lord, but if we are humble before God and man, then we cannot be defeated because...

God Gives Grace to the Humble

It should be obvious that God will not give us grace while we are still proud. Why? Because He will allow no flesh to glory in His presence. He desires us to be thoroughly emptied of ourselves. The single requirement for grace is humility. But what is grace? Grace is more than just a theological term used to describe how we are saved. Grace is the power of God at work in my life to do what cannot be done in my own strength. Grace is energizing and proactive. When I have reached the end of myself then Grace Himself takes over and does what I am unable to do. In the first place, what I cannot do is save myself, and so I trust in the Grace of God, Jesus Christ, to save me. But Grace will not only bring me through the Gate; He will bring me down the Path. Grace does not just get me started in the right direction, but goes along with me every step of the way; for Grace is a Man!

When we cease doing what we cannot do, then He begins to do what we cannot. The problem is that we still think we can do so many things. We must learn sooner, rather than later, that "apart from Me you can do nothing" (Jn. 15:5b). Nothing! But it is human nature to try and do it ourselves. This human nature is the flesh. It prevents us from entering into Grace. God cannot save someone who is still trying to save themselves. Similarly, God cannot do what we are still trying to do. He will wait – weeks, months, or years – until we have exhausted our strength. When our strength is completely gone and we finally go to Him in weakness, then He becomes our strength and we find Grace is there to do the impossible. Then we know it was not us, but the Lord. All praise goes to Him, and we retain nothing for ourselves.

See how many times the disciples tried to correct the Lord. See how many times they argued with the Lord. See how many times their thoughts contradicted the Master. See how many times they urged Him to take action. And the Lord, ever patient, would correct them. In every case we see that He is the Lord, and they are the disciples. The roles must never be confused. He is the Master, and we are His servants. He is the Teacher, and we are His students. He is the Director, and we are His employees. He is the Leader, and we are His followers. We do not command Him, but He commands us. We do not direct Him, but He directs us. We do not teach Him, but He teaches us. We do not lead Him, but He leads us. He was not created for us, but we were created for Him. He does not serve us according to our pleasure, but we serve Him according to His pleasure.

So we must be adjusted to Him, and not the other way around. The Lord will never apologize to us and say, "I'm sorry, I was wrong. We'll do it your way." How laughable! How absurd! But we often live as if we expect Him to do that very thing. We have not humbled ourselves.

All those who want power with God must come to see that His power is released through our weakness (cf. 2 Cor. 12:9). Do realize that you are weak whether you admit it or not, but the power of humility is in recognizing and agreeing before God that we really can do nothing ourselves. God's power is not for those with natural charisma, talent, leadership skills, education, training, or "connections." God is not looking for volunteers to serve at their own convenience as their schedule permits, but calls for disciples who will give up everything and lay down their lives. The flesh counts for nothing in spiritual matters.

God's power is not revealed to us when we are proud, but when we are humble. Any demonstration of "power" manifesting itself through a proud man or a proud woman is, quite simply, not from God and cannot be trusted. Spiritual gifts may be counterfeited, but spiritual fruit cannot be faked. We will know the false from the true by their fruit, not their gifts (Mt. 7:20). Meekness is an essential quality of spiritual fruit (Gal. 5:23). Gifts may accompany fruit, but gifts can never substitute for fruit.

The secret, then, is to...

Submit Yourselves Therefore to God

Do we need the power of God today? Do we seek the Life of the Lord today? Do we desire Him to have the preeminence in our lives today? Do we long for Him today? Then now is the time for us to be unconditionally and wholeheartedly surrendered to Him. We need not drag the process out for several days and weeks, months and years. "If anyone would come after me, let him deny himself and take up his cross daily and follow me" (Lk. 9:23). Do it today, do it now. If we must daily take up the Cross anyway, let us bow our head and give up the ghost instead of struggling to stay alive, which only prolongs our agony. The secret to overcoming is dying daily.

If God gives Grace to the humble, then we should live a surrendered life so we can receive grace. Die to Self, die to effort, die to trying, die to scheming. Stop wrestling, stop fighting, stop squirming, stop arguing, stop reasoning, stop bargaining, stop all that and just surrender... yield, give up, and lay down before Him!

Humility is not some outward show, but a heart attitude that says in effect, "I will not resist the dealings of God. I will not argue with the Lord. I will not insist upon my own way. I recognize and admit that apart from Him I can do nothing. I am finished. Lord, I look to You to do in me and through me what I cannot do."

Friends, if we truly mean that when we say it, then we will naturally spend more time praying, more time in the Word, more time ministering to God, because we will realize that we do not know anything and we cannot do anything without hearing from Him. If Christ is to have the preeminence in all things, then right here is where it begins. Humility is offering no resistance to the dealings of the Lord with us.

When we are submitted to the Lord, we find Grace. We find peace. We find rest. All things are in His hands, and He does all things well. We need not fear what any devil or any man can do to us. To be submitted to the Lord is to be under His care, under His guidance, under His power, under His protection.

Whom shall I fear? What can man do to me? What can the devil do to me? If I have humbled myself beneath the mighty hand of God then He will exalt me in due season; He will justify me; He will defend me; He will fight for me. If our submission to God is complete, if our surrender to the Lord is total, then victory is assured. We will...

Resist the Devil and He Will Flee

So many times we try to resist, but we are defeated. Why? Simply because we attempt to resist the devil before we have first submitted ourselves to God. There is a proper order that must be observed without fail: "Submit yourselves therefore to God. Resist the devil, and he will flee from you" (Jam. 4:7). First, we must understand the principle of God resisting the proud but giving grace to the humble. This is the foundation of everything we do.

Second, the word "therefore" signifies that those who learn this principle will act upon it accordingly. If they understand the truth just stated, they will submit "therefore" to God.

Third, as a result of their submitting to God, they will find that the devil flees whenever and wherever they offer him resistance. The word "flee" means "to run away in terror." How wonderful! How delicious to see the devil running from us in terror, instead of the other way around! That should be the normal experience of all Christians. That is the normal Christian life; a Life that overcomes.

The whole object of satan is to bring us down from the heavenly places in Christ (Eph. 2:6) and entangle us in some kind of earthly, fleshly thing that saps us of our strength and diminishes spiritual authority. Knowing this, the Lord has us pray daily, "Deliver us from evil" (Mt. 6:13ff). That is to say, "Deliver us from the earthly, the fleshly, the worldly, the carnal, the selfish, the natural, the human, where satan has influence to work evil against us. Deliver us from all that hinders and distracts us, and bring us into the Kingdom of Your dear Son so that we may walk in Spirit and Truth, in the heavenly places, demonstrating Your preeminence over all things below." Brothers and sisters, praying in this way is what it means to resist the devil. He cannot stand before us when we take the high ground and maintain the Lord's Testimony.

If we grow impatient and fall into the flesh then we become weaker. To react in the flesh diminishes spiritual authority, and this must be avoided at all costs. Allowing the flesh to have its way for only a moment guarantees defeat against a spiritual adversary. "We worship God in the Spirit, and rejoice in Christ Jesus, and have no confidence in the flesh" (Phil. 3:3). To lose all confidence in the flesh is to take the higher ground of the Spirit. To meet flesh with flesh means the victory will go to the strongest, and there is always someone stronger than you according to the flesh. Instead, if people come against you in the flesh, then let them come against you. If they wish to rail and argue with you according to the flesh, do not respond in kind. If they attack you without cause, let them attack, because the fleshly, the carnal, the natural, cannot defeat the spiritual. The one who is submitted to the Lord has authority over those who remain unsubmitted to Him. Flesh is overruled by Spirit. Hate is overruled by Love. Darkness is overruled by Light. Death is overruled by Life. Earth is overruled by Heaven. "He who comes from above is above all" (Jn. 3:31ff).

We offer no resistance, no defense, no argument, no justification to people who mean us harm. We do not wrestle against flesh and blood (Eph. 6:12a). We resist satan, not the person. We stand against the devil, taking no action against the instruments that the devil uses. We submit to God, we offer no resistance to man, but we stand firm against the spiritual adversary. Outwardly, before others, we appear weak. But inwardly, before God, we are strong. "For though we walk in the flesh, we are not waging war according to the flesh. For the weapons of our warfare are not of the flesh but have divine power to destroy strongholds" (2 Cor. 10:3,4). If we war after the flesh then we are emptied of spiritual strength. If we war after the Spirit then we are emptied of fleshly strength. Which will you have: spiritual authority, or fleshly power? You can have either one you want, but you cannot have both.

We face perilous, dangerous times. The secret of spiritual power to see us through these times is humility. Our own strength will fail us. Brothers and sisters, since we cannot avoid weakness, we may as well embrace it and make the best possible use of it. Let us accept the dealings of the Holy Spirit with us and offer no resistance to Him. "Humble yourselves before the Lord, and he will exalt you" (Jam. 4:10). Amen.

"There are those who have a life they never live. They have come to Christ and thanked Him only for what He did, but do not live in the power of who He is."

~ W. Ian Thomas

Chapter Seven

Crucified With Christ

"I have been crucified with Christ. It is no longer I who live, but Christ who lives in me. And the life I now live in the flesh I live by faith in the Son of God, who loved me and gave himself for me." (Galatians 2:20)

The doctors and the psychiatrists were stumped. Their patient had been admitted to the mental hospital for being delusional. Specifically, this man believed he was Jesus Christ. Not just metaphorically or spiritually; he actually believed he was the Son of God. How do you help a person like this?

A very gifted doctor with an excellent reputation was called in to see what he could do for the man. When he walked into the patient's room, the doctor asked, "Are you Jesus Christ?" The man replied, "Yes, my brother, how can I help you?" Excusing himself, the doctor left the room and came back in with a measuring tape. He asked the patient to stand with his arms stretched straight out from his sides, at which point the doctor used the measuring tape and carefully recorded the width of the patient's outstretched arms from fingertip to fingertip, then did the same from the top of his head to the bottom of his feet. He then left again, leaving the patient bewildered and concerned. Finally the doctor reappeared, this time with two pieces of wood, cut to the appropriate measurements, and began to nail them together in the shape of a cross. "What are you doing?" the patient asked nervously. The doctor replied, "You are Jesus Christ, right?" "Yes..." the patient said (but with a little less enthusiasm this time). "Then you know why I'm here," the doctor said quietly, but firmly, and continued constructing the cross. Suddenly the patient had a "breakthrough" and confessed that there must be some mistake, because he was not Jesus Christ after all.

When confronted with the call of the Cross, disciples of Jesus may experience a similar reluctance to follow in His footsteps. What does it really mean to be crucified with Christ? Thankfully, God does not ask us to submit to physical crucifixion in order to prove that we are disciples of Jesus. When Jesus tells us to take up our Cross and follow Him, He is not telling us that we must pay the penalty for our sins. Thank God that Jesus has paid the penalty for us! Taking up the Cross, for us, is adopting a spiritual attitude of self-denial, of surrender, and of yielding all that we have and all that we are to God. Although that aspect of the Cross occurs in us day by day and moment by moment, what Christ accomplished through His death on the Cross is finished, complete, and settled once and for all. This finished work of the Cross is the basis upon which we can take up the Cross daily and follow after Him. It is this aspect of the Cross – the finished work – that we now turn our attention to.

Identification With Christ

Paul says something very peculiar in Galatians 2:20: "I have been crucified with Christ. It is no longer I who live, but Christ who lives in me." Does Paul mean to say that he was physically there with Christ on the Cross when Jesus died? We know that Jesus was crucified between two thieves and that Paul was probably not even present at the actual, historical event of the crucifixion of Christ.

Then, Paul says that even though he was crucified, he lives. Does Paul mean to say that he was raised from the dead with Jesus also? If so, why have we not heard about this before now? Finally he says he is not really living at all, but Christ lives in him. To the natural mind, of course, this all sounds very strange. This is why we must discern spiritual things spiritually.

It should be obvious that Paul is talking about something other than a physical crucifixion and a physical death, burial, and resurrection. Although he says, "I was crucified with Christ" he does not mean that he was present with Christ in the flesh at the moment of crucifixion; instead, he intends to show us something much more profound. We will soon discover that this experience of being crucified with Christ is not unique to the apostle Paul, but is true of every born-again child of God. Not only Paul, but all disciples of Jesus have been crucified with Christ.

How is this possible? The Bible says that there is an invisible but very powerful union that exists between Jesus and all His disciples; they are one Body. It is a spiritual union. This spiritual union forms the basis of our relationship and fellowship with Christ. Jesus says, "I am the True Vine... live in Me, and I will live in you" (Jn. 15:1,4a). Jesus compares this union to a vine that has many branches. Each branch lives in union with the vine. The same life flowing in the vine is also flowing in the branches. Jesus says He is the True Vine, and we are His branches. This is spiritual union. As branches, we can only grow and produce spiritual fruit so long as we continue to live, dwell in, abide, and be part of the Vine. So then, union with God is not the reward for spirituality; it is the basis of spirituality.

With this analogy we can now understand what Paul means when we look at some of his other statements. He tells the Corinthians that "He who is joined to the Lord becomes one spirit with him" (1 Cor. 6:17). To the Ephesians, Paul compares this spiritual union to the union that exists between a man and a woman when they are married: "And the two shall become one flesh. This mystery is profound, and I am saying that it refers to Christ and the [Ekklesia]" (Eph. 5:31b,32).

Certainly this is a great mystery. How God is able to make us one spirit with Jesus is beyond human knowledge. But this we know: however it is accomplished, it has its beginning in the Cross. The Cross is the starting point of our union with Christ. In the Cross, God sees us in the place of Christ and sees Christ in the place of us. That is to say, in the Cross, all our sinfulness is attributed to Christ, and all His righteousness is attributed to us.

How wonderful for us – but how terrible for Him! Yet this is God's Way, and the Bible refers to it as identification:

> For our sake he made him to be sin who knew no sin, so that in him we might become the righteousness of God. (2 Cor. 5:21)

The Bible never identifies us as being one with Jesus in His preexistence with God, or in His birth, or in His sinless life on earth. But when Jesus submitted to the Cross He indentified with us by taking on our sins and accepting the penalty just the same as if He had sinned Himself. In the same manner, when we submit to the Cross, God identifies us with Christ just the same as if we were sinless. Jesus becomes our wisdom, righteousness, sanctification, and redemption (1 Cor. 1:30). It does not say that He gives these things to us, it says He is these things to us.

Was Jesus crucified for His sins? No, He was crucified for our sins. Are we now wise, righteous, sanctified, and redeemed because of anything we have done? No, God simply identifies us together with Christ, as if we were crucified together with Him. He loses everything and we gain everything. This is why salvation begins with repentance, surrender, and faith in Christ and His finished work on the Cross. It cannot be accomplished otherwise. What a glorious Lord we have!

Being "In Christ"

You may wonder how this union with Jesus was accomplished. I do not have the answer to that, but I consider it to be so because God says it is so. God placed us in Christ. I do not fully understand how He did this, but I know that He did it, and I thank God for it. The Bible says that "because of [God] you are in Christ Jesus" (1 Cor. 1:30a). Disciples of Jesus are one with Christ because God has placed us there. We are in Christ, and Christ is in us. We may not understand how this can be so, but it is so. We are spiritually one with Christ. This oneness, this union, this partnership and fellowship with Him is the basis of our spiritual life and our walk with God.

Passengers in a commercial airliner must entrust themselves to the plane when they wish to fly somewhere. They place themselves in the jet, and once there, their destiny (for better or for worse) is linked to the plane. If the plane rises to 30,000 feet, the passengers rise also. If the plane crashes, the passengers crash right along with it. When the plane arrives at its destination, the passengers arrive at the exact same moment. Is it possible for the plane to arrive in Seattle but for the passengers on the plane to arrive in Dallas? Or could some of the plane's passengers arrive in Miami while the rest of the passengers arrive in Denver? Of course not. Is it possible for the plane to arrive one hour or one minute or even one second before or after the passengers arrive? By no means. All the passengers who are in the plane arrive whenever and wherever the plane arrives. In the same way, when God placed us in Christ, He forever linked us to Christ's death, burial, resurrection, ascension, and being seated in the heavenlies. So God considers us to have been crucified, dead, buried, resurrected, ascended, and seated as well. It cannot be otherwise. So long as we remain in Him (Jn. 15:5) our destinies are linked.

I once placed a $20 bill inside of a book. I then misplaced the book. What happened to the $20 bill? The bill was lost when the book was lost. The bill and the book were linked together because I placed one inside the other. In order to find the bill I had to find the book. Once I found the book, I also found the bill. In like manner, God has placed us in Christ. When Christ was crucified, we were also crucified. When Christ was raised, we were also raised. The two have become one, and what is true of Him is true of all those who are one with Him.

Now, follow me closely here. Before my father married my mother and conceived me, he was in a serious automobile accident. You ask, did he survive the accident? You know very well that he did survive, because I am alive and able to write these words. But had my father died at the age of sixteen, I would have died also, because I was still in my father. His death would have been my death; and not my death only, but also the death of my children, and their children, all the way down the line. We would have all died together with him, having never even lived. But his life, his survival, his overcoming the accident was just as much my life, my survival, and my overcoming. His testimony of life and overcoming death is verified by my life, and the life of my children, and on down the line. Spiritually speaking, this is similar to what God has done for us by placing us in Christ. Christ was crucified, dead, buried, resurrected, ascended, and seated; and since we were in Him when it all happened, God considers it to have happened to us as well. We who are His children now share in the very life of Christ, and each of us bear witness to the resurrection and overcoming of Christ. When God raised Him from the dead, He raised us from the dead as well.

The key to all of this, of course, is to see ourselves in the exact same way that God sees us. We must see that God has made us one with Christ; only then can we say, along with Paul, "I am crucified with Christ" and experience the reality of the fact. Once we see that then it will be very easy to see that we who were crucified with Christ were dead, buried, resurrected, ascended, and seated together with Him also. Tremendous benefits accrue to those who God has made one with Christ, for when we are made one with Him then our spiritual history becomes linked with His. We are "blessed with every spiritual blessing... in Christ" (Eph. 1:3). In ourselves? Never! Only in Him!

The Cross: A Settled Fact

The Cross we now bear as disciples of Jesus speaks of daily submitting ourselves to a spiritual principle that says, "He must increase, but I must decrease" (Jn. 3:30). Not so with the cross that Jesus died on; for on that cross, Jesus was crucified once, and one time was enough. "For by a single offering he has perfected for all time those who are sanctified" (Heb. 10:14, RSV). Jesus does not need to be crucified over and over again; it is a settled, accomplished fact. When He said, "It is finished" (Jn. 19:30) He indicated that there was no more sacrifice to be made. The Greek phrase for 'it is finished' is a single word: *teleō*. It is an accounting term that means "paid in full." Hallelujah! So we do not need to be crucified for our many sins, nor must we ask Jesus to be crucified over and over again. Thank God, the debt has been paid in full for us through Christ. His death was our death, and His life is now our life:

> For if while we were enemies we were reconciled to God by the death of his Son, much more, now that we are reconciled, shall we be saved by his life. More than that, we also rejoice in God through our Lord Jesus Christ, through whom we have now received reconciliation. (Rom. 5:10,11)

On the surface it seems as if Jesus died for me so that I would not have to die; but that is not exactly so. The truth is that Jesus died as me, and so now God considers me to have already died. God has not delivered us from death, He has delivered us through death and by death. Were God to deliver Jesus from death then the Cross would have been rendered null and void. No death would have occurred, and without a death there would have been no resurrection. But thank God, Jesus embraced the Cross and tasted death on our behalf so that we can join Him in Resurrection Life and never die again:

> For the love of Christ controls us, because we have concluded this: that **one has died for all, therefore all have died**; and he died for all, that those who live might no longer live for themselves but for him who for their sake died and was raised. (2 Cor. 5:14,15)

He died for all; therefore, all have died. This is why the Cross is so powerful. It represents our oneness with Christ. Apart from this Cross we have no connection and no union with Jesus. But because of the Cross, Paul states that God "has made us accepted in the Beloved" (Eph. 1:6). This means we are acceptable to God because we are in the only One Who can ever be acceptable to Him: "This is My Beloved Son, with Whom I am well pleased" (Mt. 3:17). We are not acceptable to God just because we call ourselves Christians or because we live a good life and do good things. This is unacceptable to God because our righteousness is "filthy rags" (Isa. 64:6) compared to Jesus Christ the Righteous One. And so, God places us in Christ. Since we are in the Beloved, we are accepted because He is accepted. This is why there is no other Way, Truth, or Life outside of, or apart from Christ (Jn. 14:6). No other way is acceptable; no other way is even possible. Others may try but they must eventually bow down and submit to the truth: "Without Me you can do nothing" (Jn. 15:5b). But the one who has been placed in Christ can say, "I can do all things through Christ Who strengthens me" (Php. 4:13).

Scripture bears witness to a most amazing spiritual truth: that disciples of Jesus are the crucified, dead, buried, resurrected, ascended, and seated Branches of a crucified, dead, buried, resurrected, ascended, and seated Vine. So let us turn now to these Scriptures and trace each aspect of this wonderful mystery.

Crucified With Christ

> We know that our old self was crucified **with him** in order that the body of sin might be brought to nothing, so that we would no longer be enslaved to sin. (Rom. 6:6)

> I have been crucified **with Christ**. It is no longer I who live, but Christ who lives in me. (Gal. 2:20a)

> Those who **belong to** Christ Jesus have crucified the flesh with its passions and desires. (Gal. 5:24)

> But far be it from me to boast except in the cross of our Lord Jesus Christ, **by which** the world has been crucified to me, and I to the world. (Gal. 6:14)

As I taught on this wonderful fact many years ago, I noticed a brother was taking notes. Afterwards he showed me what he had written down. He wrote, "The flesh has to die; I must crucify my flesh." But that is not what the Scripture says, and that is not what I taught. Scripture says that those who belong to Christ Jesus have crucified (past tense) the flesh with its passions and desires. No one can commit suicide by crucifixion. Someone else must nail us to the Cross. The flesh cannot crucify itself. Jesus has already done what we could not do. The sooner we stop trying to crucify ourselves, the sooner we can boast in the finished work of the Cross and actually witness the evidence of it in our lives.

Notice that Paul does not merely say that Jesus was crucified for us. That is certainly true in and of itself. But there is more. Not only was Jesus crucified for us, He was crucified as us. God considers us to have been crucified as surely as if we were there receiving the nails in our hands and feet. We have been crucified together with Him because God placed us in Him the moment He was crucified.

Died With Christ

> Do you not know that all of us who have been baptized **into Christ Jesus** were baptized **into** his death? (Rom. 6:3)

> Now if we have died **with Christ**, we believe that we will also live **with him.** (Rom. 6:8a)

> So you also must consider yourselves dead to sin and alive to God **in Christ Jesus.** (Rom. 6:11)

> Likewise, my brothers, you also have died to the law **through the body of Christ.** (Rom. 7:4a)

> We have concluded this: that **one has died for all**, therefore all have died. (2. Cor. 5:14)

> If **with Christ** you died to the elemental spirits of the world, why, as if you were still alive in the world, do you submit to regulations? (Col. 2:20)

> For you have died, and your life is hidden **with Christ** in God. (Col. 3:3)

Why does the Bible say that we died with Christ? Because we were crucified with Him. When He was crucified, we were crucified. And no one survives a crucifixion. Therefore, when Christ died, we died together with Him.

Buried With Christ

> We were buried therefore **with him** by baptism into death. (Rom. 6:4a)

> Having been buried **with him** in baptism. (Col. 2:12a)

We do not bury someone unless we are absolutely sure that they are dead. Ordinarily that would be the end of the story: a life, a death, and a burial. But we have been joined to One Who has overcome death. This is the whole purpose of the Cross. If we remain in union with Him through crucifixion, death and burial, then we will certainly remain in union with Him through all that follows after. So we have also been...

Resurrected With Christ

> For if we have been united with him in a death like his, we shall certainly be **united with him** in a resurrection like his. (Rom. 6:5)

> Even when we were dead in our trespasses, [God] made us alive **together with Christ**. (Eph. 2:5a)

> And you, who were dead in your trespasses and the uncircumcision of your flesh, God made alive **together with him**, having forgiven us all our trespasses. (Col. 2:13)

If we share in His death then we will share in His life. How could it be otherwise? What is true of the Vine is true of the Branches that are part of the Vine. It would be impossible for the Vine to be raised while the Branches that are part of the Vine to remain buried. So long as the Vine and the Branches are one, they share in both the suffering and in the glory that is revealed afterwards.

In the same way, when God made us one spirit together with Christ on the Cross, His intention was for us to experience both the Crucifixion and the Resurrection. So Paul says that if we suffer with Him, then we will reign with Him (2 Tim. 2:12). Again, we see the purpose of the Cross. If we refuse to join Him in suffering then we cannot hope to join Him in ruling. If we refuse the Crucified Death then we cannot have the Resurrected Life.

But there is yet more. When Jesus was raised from the dead, He did not continue to live on the earth as He had previously. He ascended to Heaven. So let us ask: if we have been crucified, dead, buried, and resurrected with Christ, have we also ascended and been seated together with Him? Or should we see this merely as a future event? Certainly there is a future fulfillment we look forward to, but the basis of that future fulfillment has its roots in a present reality: that because of the Cross, we are already...

Ascended and Seated With Christ

> [God] raised us up **with him** and seated us **with him** in the heavenly places **in Christ Jesus**. (Eph. 2:6)

> The one who conquers, I will grant him to sit **with me** on my throne, **as I also** conquered and sat down with my Father on his throne. (Rev. 3:21)

There is no higher place in the universe than to be seated in the heavenlies at the right hand of God. Who or what can touch you there? Jesus is Lord of all, preeminent over all, and seated in His throne. And now – glorious truth! – we who are in Him have been raised, ascended, and seated together with Him.

Note the past tense of Ephesians 2:6 and the present tense of Revelation 3:21. This is not something for us to enjoy at some point in the distant future; it is something God has already done for us together with

Christ when He raised Him up from the dead, raised Him up from the earth and seated Him at His own right hand. Spiritually speaking, that is our position as well: ascended, above the earth, triumphant over all enemies!

How is this possible? Trace it as far back as you can, beginning with where you are "now." You are seated together with Christ because you ascended together with Christ. You ascended together with Christ because you were resurrected and made alive together with Christ. You were resurrected and made alive together with Christ because you were buried together with Christ. You were buried together with Christ because you died together with Christ. You died together with Christ because you were crucified together with Christ.

This brings us back to Galatians 2:20, for that is where it all began: "I was crucified with Christ." Back to the Cross! For the Cross is where the two became one. The Cross is where God places us in Christ so that we are joined to Him and become one spirit. The Cross is the means by which we enter into this enduring, living union with Christ.

Do you see, dear friend, that victory, conquering, ruling, reigning, and overcoming is only possible through the Cross? Because of the Cross we have been made one with Him Who overcame all things. His victory is our victory. But we cannot experience the Victory of that Life if we do not embrace the seeming defeat of that Cross.

So long as we try to "rise up" and "claim victory" over this thing or that thing in our own strength, we will remain bound to the earth. "No one has ascended into heaven except he who descended from heaven, the Son of Man" (Jn. 3:13). No man has ascended because no man can ascend. Rest assured that if it were possible, someone would have done it! But just as we cannot make ourselves acceptable to God on the basis of anything we have done, so too we cannot ascend and seat ourselves at the right hand of God. We are accepted only in the Beloved; we are saved only in the Beloved; and only in the Beloved can we be raised from the dead, ascended and be seated in the heavenlies.

Reckoning and Reality

Some may say, "But I don't feel as though I am seated with Christ in the heavenlies. I do not have any sense of victory. I see what God says and I want to believe, but my experience contradicts what God says. So I do not know how to live this out in a practical way."

I understand. Your experience is like the poor man who suddenly had a large inheritance of money deposited into his bank account. The money was his, free and clear. The poor man received a bank statement every month but he never opened the statement because he "knew" he had no money. So he continued to live in poverty, worrying about how to feed and clothe himself and how to pay his bills. Finally, out of sheer curiosity, he opened his bank statement one month and saw that he was worth millions of dollars.

Most would be ecstatic, but he had a poverty mentality and couldn't believe what he saw. The bank said he was rich; but he "knew" he was poor. Had he simply believed what the bank statement said he could have acted upon it and pretty soon his experience would have lined up with reality. But he couldn't believe it, and since he wouldn't believe it, he never acted upon it.

In Christ are hidden all the treasures of wisdom and knowledge (Col. 2:3). Most people are like the poor man who never opened his bank statement. They never open the Word of God to discover all that they have inherited in Christ. Their heavenly statement of account lies there collecting dust from week to week while they struggle along in spiritual poverty due to their own ignorance. What a tragedy that is! And totally unnecessary!

"Yes, but if only someone had told him of his inheritance he might not have been so ignorant of it!" Really? The bank told him every month of his inheritance but he paid no attention! And when he finally did open up the statement and read of his great wealth, he still refused to believe it! Do you read the Word of God? Do you read books on living the Christian life? Reading is not enough. Listening is not enough. Very little is accomplished through mere reading and listening; it takes some actual believing to go along with the reading and the listening! "All things are possible to the one who believes." No doubt you have read these Scriptures numerous times; but for them to become a living reality they must be spiritually seen and believed. And once they are sincerely believed then they will be acted upon.

How then do you act upon these Scriptures? If the poor man could have suspended his unbelief long enough to ask the bank for some money, then he would have received all the proof he needed of his inheritance. So, for your first action, I ask you to suspend your unbelief and go to God. Go to the One Who says He has provided you with a rich inheritance in Christ and ask for a withdrawal. Do not be like the rich, poor man who refused to believe. Ask God to open your eyes to this glorious Christ and the wonder of His Cross! Ask Him to give you "the spirit of wisdom and revelation in the knowledge of Him" (Eph. 1:17).

Then, with "the eyes of your understanding being enlightened" (Eph 1:18) you can now return to your "bank statement" there in the Word of God and see riches that you never saw before. It is important that you "reconcile your checkbook" by writing down every single deposit you discover there in the Scriptures. If you fail to do this then you cannot truly appreciate how much wealth you are sitting on. Whenever you uncover something, write it down and store it away. Before long you will begin to cry out, "Oh, the depth of the riches and wisdom and knowledge of God" (Rom. 11:33a)!

Now the next step is very important: whenever you discover a new spiritual truth, and record it, you must act upon it. "Everyone then who hears these words of mine and does them will be like a wise man who built his house on the rock" (Mt. 7:24). Scriptures such as "love God and love your neighbor" are pretty straightforward. But how do you put spiritual truths and statements of fact into practice? How do you "do" Galatians 2:20? How do you act upon your being "seated with Christ?"

Very simple: just begin to live, think, and act as if it were true. Because it is true. But too many want to see if it is true before they live as if it is true. That is like saying to the fireplace, "You give me heat, and then I will put in the logs." Or like saying to the fertile ground, "You give me some corn, and then I will give you some seeds." Or like saying to the bank, "You give me some interest, and then I will invest my principal with you."

If you want heat, you put in the logs first. If you want to reap a harvest, you plant the seeds first. If you want to get a return on your investment, you have to make the investment first. In the same way, if you want to see the spiritual reality of something you have to risk looking like a fool and acting as if it is true before you experience the truth of it. Understanding, of course, that spiritual truth is true whether you believe it or not. But we are trying to get your experience to line up with the truth so that you can benefit from it. It is of no benefit to have a rich inheritance in Christ if you are ignorant of your inheritance.

For example, suppose that in your reading you discover this: "Little children, you are from God and have overcome them, for he who is in you is greater than he who is in the world" (1 Jn. 4:4). If you really believe this, will it make a difference in the way you go about your day? Will it make a difference in how you see your problems and your circumstances? Will it change the way you see spiritual warfare? Absolutely! You cannot accept this as being true and continue to live as you have always lived. Greater is He that is in me! To act upon this you simply thank God for what it says, and from that moment on, you live as though it is true – regardless of what your feelings, your circumstances, your family, your friends, or the devil says.

To enjoy the benefits of your inheritance in Christ requires faith. What is faith? Faith is simply believing that God is Who He says He is and that God will do (or has already done) what He says He will do. Faith is not believing something after you see it happen. Thomas had no trouble believing Jesus after he saw Him, but Jesus said, "You believe because you have seen; blessed are they who believe, having never seen" (Jn. 20:29).

There is usually a period of time between believing and seeing; this is where faith is tested. This is where many give up and turn back. But those who persevere and persist will be rewarded when God confirms their belief with actual, tangible results.

To see this demonstrated once more, let us go back to one truth that is particularly difficult for us to accept: "those who belong to Christ Jesus have crucified the flesh with its passions and desires." (Gal. 5:24). We see what God says, but then we look at our experience and see our flesh and see that its desires are alive and strong. So we have a choice. Either God is wrong or we are wrong. Which is it? Well, God is not wrong. So either you aren't part of Christ or you haven't truly seen this truth. But now you see it. Your heart leaps, you want to believe it, but it seems impossible...

So faith takes hold of the Word of God and says, "I'm going to believe this because God says it. Now, my circumstances say otherwise. But I am willing to look like a fool for believing God. Even if I die having never experienced this, I'm going to believe it anyway, for no other reason than simply because God says it is so. Therefore, I agree with God. I thank and praise God that I belong to Jesus, and my flesh with all its passions and desires has been crucified!"

Watchman Nee called this "reckoning." He was referring to Romans 6:11: "Reckon yourself to be dead indeed to sin, but alive to God through Jesus Christ our Lord." We do not reckon something to be so after we see it happen, but before we see it happen. What happens if, right after we reckon ourselves dead to sin, we fall back into sin? Does this nullify the Word of God? Does this make God a liar? We can become disappointed and quit (which is what most people do), or we can repent and go right back to reckoning. Here's what happens: God rewards our reckoning. He delights to see us believing in His Word when it seems impossible! And so He says, "Very well, you have believed having not seen; now you will begin to see the truth of what you have been reckoning!" And eventually we begin to see our reckoning begins to produce fruit. Sin will be broken, not just in theory, but in actual practice. Victory will be ours, not just in principle, but in fact.

This extraordinary belief in God compels Him to confirm His Word. If the Bible says I am dead to sin, and I take God at His Word, then God, Who is "watching over His Word to perform it" (Jer. 1:12), will certainly ensure that my trust in Him is not misplaced. I am not saying that we can manipulate God and compel Him to answer foolish, self-centered, misguided prayers. But we can certainly take Him at His Word and expect that He is Who He says He is and that He will do what He says He will do.

There are many things to discover in Christ. In fact, to know Him is to know how little of Him we know. Spiritual growth and maturity is the natural result of discovering something new in Christ, reckoning it to be so, living as if it is so (despite all evidence to the contrary), and then seeing our faith rewarded with tangible evidence, spiritual fruit, and practical results. There is a world of difference between reading about our victory in Christ and actually casting out devils. The space in between the spiritual truth and the practical expression of the truth is where we are growing, learning, and maturing. We will sometimes fail, make mistakes, and be sorely tempted to believe what we see and feel instead of what God says. But if we persevere, victory is inevitable. The Cross cannot fail.

"The Cross is the great and consummate point of everything, which gives meaning to everything else, both the person, the work, and the teaching; the Cross it is that gives power to everything else."

~ T. Austin-Sparks

Chapter Eight

The Two-Fold Work of the Cross

"Christ also suffered for you, leaving you an example, so that you might follow in his steps." (1 Peter 2:21)

If we were to ask a Christian, "Have you accepted the work of the Cross?" Many of them would say yes. If you then asked them what the work of the Cross is, they would respond by saying that the work of the Cross is the crucifixion of the Lord Jesus for the sins of the world.

While this is true enough, it can be misleading. A better question to ask is, "Have you accepted the two-fold work of the Cross?" Try this out on a few Christians and you will probably get a puzzled reply along the lines of, "What is the two-fold work of the Cross?" That is because most people are only familiar with one side of the Cross, not both sides.

For many years I was only taught one aspect of the Cross – that is, the cross on which Jesus died for me. That is all I knew, and so that is all I taught. On this cross He was crucified as my substitute. He laid down His life for me. His precious blood was poured out for the forgiveness of my sins. Not only that, but the Bible says that God laid on Jesus the iniquity of us all. John the Baptist called Him, "The Lamb of God Who takes away the sins of the whole world."

By identifying with His sacrificial death, He becomes our Substitute. We enter into His finished work. We are made one with Him there on the cross. Thank God that we do not have to pay this debt, for it has been paid for us. We do not have to go to the cross and be crucified for our sins.

I would suggest that almost every Christian is familiar with this aspect of the Cross. It is the foundation of evangelicalism and the basis of millions of sermons to millions of believers. It is the truth, and we thank God for the truth whenever it is proclaimed.

However, there is another side to this Cross, another dimension of the same truth, which is not as well-known, and is hardly preached at all. As a result, many believers are content to embrace the "Sinner's Cross" – that is, they have confessed Jesus as Savior, and they understand and accept Him as their Substitute. It is certainly true that Jesus is our Substitute, and that He died on the cross for us. But as we have said, there is a two-fold work of the Cross.

Peter alludes to this two-fold work when he writes, "Christ also suffered for you, leaving you an example, so that you might follow in his steps." Christ suffered for us; that is the first aspect. But He also left us an example; that is the second aspect.

So the work of the Cross is two-fold. Firstly, Jesus is our Substitute. Secondly, He is our Example. In the first case, He took up the Cross. In the second case, I

The Two-Fold Work of the Cross

take up the Cross. The first work of the Cross is for the Sinner; the second work of the Cross is for the Disciple.

Jesus said that the way to Life is through a narrow Gate and a difficult Path. The Gate is only the beginning of the journey; it is not the destination. So we must have both the Gate and the Path. One is not complete without the other. Once we are through the Gate (Christ's work of the Cross) then there is a Path for us to walk (of taking up my Cross daily). The Gate makes it possible for us to walk the Path, but the Gate is incomplete without the Path. Fullness of Life and maturity is at the end of the Path, not at the beginning. The "Sinner's Cross" is the Gate. Because Jesus is my Substitute, I can now walk the Path. The "Disciple's Cross" is the Path. Now I am following His example. Can you see the difference?

Jesus says the way to Life is through a Narrow Gate and a Difficult Path. The Narrow Gate is Christ. It is Narrow because He is the Only Way. But why is the Path so difficult? Partly because it is much easier, much more appealing, to accept Jesus as a Substitute than to accept Him as an Example. Stated differently, it is much more appealing to accept Jesus as Savior than to accept Him as Lord. With a simple prayer I can acknowledge Him as my Substitute and Savior. But to make Him my Example and my Lord, to actually walk in His footsteps, is not so appealing.

Why? In the first case I simply embrace the "Sinner's Cross" and everything is done for me. But in the second case I must take up the "Disciple's Cross" and actually follow in the steps of my Master. It only takes a moment to pass through the Gate, but the Path takes a lifetime of walking.

Peter wrote of this two-fold work of the Cross, but we see in Matthew 16 that he did not always have this understanding. In Matthew 16 we see Jesus as our Substitute and our Example all in one chapter. First there is Jesus as the Substitute. He begins to show His disciples that He must go to Jerusalem, suffer many things, be killed, and raised the third day. For His sins? No, for our sins. So in this He is our Substitute.

Peter, taking offense over this, pulls Jesus aside and begins to rebuke Him. Imagine! Peter is rebuking the Lord Jesus over this issue of the Cross. It is, indeed, a difficult thing to comprehend. But Jesus turns and rebukes Peter, "Yes, it will be so. I will go to Jerusalem and die for the sins of the world. I must complete My substitutionary work."

But the two-fold work of the Cross goes deeper than the physical death of Jesus. And so Jesus immediately begins to speak to them, not about HIS Cross, but about THEIR Cross:

> Then Jesus told his disciples, "If anyone would come after me, let him deny himself and take up his cross and follow me. For whoever would save his life will lose it, but whoever loses his life for my sake will find it." (Mt. 16:24,25)

Peter objected to the death of the Lord Jesus and wanted to prevent His crucifixion. The Lord Jesus responded that not only must the Master be crucified,

The Two-Fold Work of the Cross

but anyone who desired to follow after the Master would, of necessity, have to take up their Cross as well.

Peter eventually learned this lesson, and it is time we learned it as well. Jesus is both my Substitute and my Example. Jesus is both my Savior and my Lord. Jesus is both the Narrow Gate and the Difficult Path.

If there is any doubt as to the reason for a lack of power, a lack of joy, a lack of faithfulness, a lack of Spirit-and-Truth today, we need only examine a person's ultimate attitude towards the Cross. Is the Cross, to them, something that Jesus saved them from, or something that Jesus saved them for? The fruit, or the lack thereof, tells the whole story. For there never will be, and there never can be, any fruitfulness apart from embracing the two-fold work of the Cross.

The question will of course arise: can Jesus be Savior, but not be Lord? Can I accept the salvation but not the discipleship? Can I enter the Gate but not walk the Path? And the underlying concern is really this: can I pray the Sinner's Prayer, live any way I please, and still go to heaven when I die?

The question itself is very revealing in the ones who ask it. Consider that it takes two beams to make a cross; one beam is not enough. If we accept only half of the two-fold work of the Cross then we have not truly embraced the Cross. If we continue to preach an easy Gospel and bring sinners to an easy Jesus by having them pray an easy prayer, then we are guilty of propagating another gospel: a false gospel, a Gate without a Path.

The Rich Young Ruler came to Jesus with the exact same concern: what must I do to inherit eternal life? His primary concern was going to heaven when he died. For many Christians that is the ultimate objective and the motivation behind everything they do. In actuality, Jesus said comparatively little about "going to heaven when you die." But He had quite a bit to say about being obedient to the will of God and producing fruit while you're still living here on earth.

To the Rich Young Ruler who wanted to be saved, Jesus offered discipleship, not salvation:

> And Jesus, looking at him, loved him, and said to him, "You lack one thing: go, sell all that you have and give to the poor, and you will have treasure in heaven; and come, follow me." Disheartened by the saying, he went away sorrowful, for he had great possessions. And Jesus looked around and said to his disciples, "How difficult it will be for those who have wealth to enter the kingdom of God!" (Mk. 10:21-23)

Not "how easy for them to enter the Kingdom of God", but "how difficult it is". The two-fold work of the Cross is a hard saying for rich and for poor alike. Many turn away sad and sorrowful at the thought of taking up the Cross as a disciple. For that reason, only the first half of the two-fold work of the Cross is preached.

I suspect that the Rich Young Ruler would have eagerly accepted Jesus as his Substitute – because the subtle implication is that since Jesus died on the Cross, I won't have to die! But like all the other suggestions of the adversary, this too is only a partial truth. For the whole truth is that the work of the Cross is two-fold, and we can embrace both, or neither, but we cannot keep one and discard the other.

You may be concerned that if we make salvation contingent on discipleship then fewer people would get saved. That's exactly the point. This is precisely what Jesus meant when He said, "Few find it" (Mt. 7:14b).

So what are we to do? Should we continue to give false comfort to those who are unwilling to take up their Cross, deny Self, and follow Jesus? By no means. Instead, let us endeavor to show others, by example, that the only way to Life is through Death; the only way to reign with Him is to suffer with Him. Not those who hear, but those who hear and put into practice, are His true disciples.

May the Lord Jesus Himself bear witness of these things, that they are true. Amen.

"Christ is the Son of God. He died to atone for men's sin, and after three days rose again. This is the most important fact in the universe. I die believing in Christ."

~ Watchman Nee

(Note found under his pillow, in prison, at his death)

Chapter Nine

The Prisoners of the Lord

"'Do you want to know the truth? The truth is that when you were young, you could dress yourself and go wherever you wanted to go. But when you are older, you too, will stretch out your hands and Someone Else will clothe you and tell you where to go and take you where you would not choose to go.' Jesus said this to show that Peter would one day be crucified, just as He had been, and would honor God in his death." (John 21:18,19, TIL)

M ost Christians who come to the Lord experience great joy when they first begin to follow Him. With this feeling of joy they can pray with great power. They can sing and worship with liberty. Whenever they pick up the Bible they instantly find spiritual nourishment. It seems as though the words on the page leap out at them. Everything about their Christian life is effortless.

In the beginning of their Christian walk these new disciples enjoy being around other believers. Going to church or participating in some kind of ministry is the greatest thrill of their lives. They are burdened for lost souls, and can witness with great boldness to everyone they meet. What they lack in experience they make up for in pure zeal.

But strangely enough, a change begins to take place after they have spent some time walking with the Lord. Prayer becomes more and more of a chore. They can go through the motions of praise and worship, but it seems very dry. When they read from the Bible they find little that interests them. If they enjoyed going to church before, now they have to force themselves to attend, and are inclined not to go at all. They seem to have lost their burden for souls and seldom open their mouth to witness. Indeed, all their former activities seem laughable to them, even hypocritical, when they consider their former state and compare it to their present state. Perhaps the church will encourage them to redouble their efforts in an attempt to restore their good feelings, but nothing seems to work.

Should we consider these Christians to be backslidden? Have they lost their first love? Has God simply forgotten all about them?

In a word, these young disciples were once able to dress themselves and go wherever they wanted to go. But now that they are older, they are being led by Another who intends to take them in a direction they would never choose on their own – because it will mean the death of Self.

The Narrow Path of Self-Denial

Since most Christians believe their spiritual life is at its highest whenever they "feel" spiritual, they deem it to be at its lowest whenever they "feel" unspiritual. In other words, as long as prayer and praise is flowing like a river then they must be doing the right thing. As long as Bible reading, church attendance, and good works are enjoyable, then they believe they are on the right track. But if ever they begin to feel uneasy, dark, or dreary in their walk they (incorrectly) believe that they have lost something of their former status as "powerful" believers.

What we must understand is that spiritual life has nothing to do with how we feel. But some disciples reason along these lines: "Today I was able to rise with the sun and pray with great feeling. My devotional reading really spoke to my heart. I am at peace and full of joy. This is the spiritual life!" But the day following, they may say to themselves, "Today I overslept and could not really enter into prayer. My devotions were dry and unsatisfying. I know I am saved, but I do not feel particularly spiritual today. I have lost my spiritual life."

Brothers and sisters, I am acquainted with enough people to know that what I am describing does not affect a small number of Christians, but is in fact the experience of many believers. They believe their spiritual life is at its highest when they feel spiritual, and believe it is at its lowest when they feel unspiritual. This is because they believe the Lord only wants positive, bright, happy, and delicious things for them. The reality is that they have mistaken a life of feeling for a life of faith.

The truth is that when we are young, we may dress ourselves and go about as we wish. But true spiritual growth is less of me, and more of Him (Jn. 3:30). The true evidence of growth is not how we feel about ourselves, or what other people judge us to be. Our spiritual walk is not the sum total of all our wonderful experiences and feelings. True growth is the decreasing of Self and the increasing of Christ. True "spiritual power" is based in weakness, not strength. True "spiritual life" is based in death: "It is no longer I who live, but Christ who lives in me." (cf. Gal. 2:20). So when we are older in the Lord, we may no longer lead ourselves, but we must stretch forth our hands and allow Another to dress us and lead us where WE would not choose to go; yet it is as necessary as it is inevitable.

One characteristic of young disciples is their ability to dress and lead themselves. They find it very easy to go out and to come in. They are zealous and full of good works. If they see a need, they move at once to fill it. If they want to go somewhere, they simply go. If they want to say something, they simply say it. If they want to do something, they simply do it. They are full of plans and pursuits.

We are not suggesting that this is necessarily wrong, but we are suggesting that this is only the beginning stage of spiritual growth. The real question is not what need do I want to fill, or where do I want to go, or what do I want to say, or what do I want to do. The question is: what satisfies the Lord? Whenever "I" do something I consider spiritual and good, it is, nevertheless, "me" who does it. Often we do what satisfies us – the Lord and His Need are seldom considered. But when we ask what satisfies the Lord, we see (in this passage at least) that the Lord is glorified when He is able to dress us and lead us where He wants us to go – with no interference from Self.

Spiritual maturity is not being able to do more or less, it is being able to do nothing of myself. God is more glorified in my "death" than in my "life." It is very difficult for people to see this. They have been told that God "hired" them and put them to work for His Kingdom (or for the "church"). If they do not report for "work" every week, then (they are told) God's Kingdom suffers loss. Instead of the Lord's easy yoke and light burden, Religion gives them a difficult yoke and a heavy burden.

Those who are young may have complete liberty to dress themselves and go wherever they please. But after some time the Lord begins to touch those things, and we find it increasingly difficult to live, move, or do anything of our own accord. Self begins to be replaced with Christ, and Someone Else begins to dress us and take us to places where we would not wish to go.

The Lord's Prisoners Are Really At Liberty, Though Bound

> I, Paul, the prisoner of the Lord, implore you... (Eph. 4:1a)

T. Austin-Sparks addressed an assembly of believers in Manila back in the 1960's. The saints there had repeatedly pressed him to come sooner, but no amount of persuasion could get him to come until he had the

Lord's direction. When he finally did arrive, he explained why he had been so long in coming: "You know, dear friends, we are the prisoners of the Lord Jesus. We cannot go where we would like to go. And we cannot move when we would like to move."

In this simple illustration we see the difference between the young and the old. The young are independent and free. If the way is blocked, they work at once to break through the blockage. They never consider that perhaps the way is blocked because they are still dressing and leading themselves. But the ones who know the Lord are not independent and free. They are restricted like a prisoner. How so? Because Someone Else decides if they will or will not go, what they will or will not say, and what they will or will not do.

There is a liberty that is really not liberty at all, it is a kind of disguised bondage. Many will proclaim themselves to be "free" when it should be clear that true freedom is not the ability to do as I please, but to be free from doing as I please; for when I do as I please, when I follow my own will and my own way, it just leads to more bondage.

On the other hand, there is a bondage that is really not bondage at all, it is a kind of disguised liberty. The prisoners of the Lord know something of this "disguised liberty." By stretching forth their arms to be dressed and led about by Another, they seem to be throwing away all their "rights." How strange, we think, that the Lord often puts His greatest ambassadors in chains – literally and figuratively. But the prisoners of

The Prisoners of the Lord

the Lord have more liberty in their "bondage" than most people have in their "liberty."

What does it mean to be the prisoner of the Lord? It means that we are not our own anymore. We do not belong to the world. We do not belong to the earth. We do not even belong to the church. We are the Lord's peculiar possession. As the prisoner of the Lord we give up all our rights. We give up our independent ways and submit ourselves to His Will and His Kingdom in all things.

Now, when we first come to the Lord, we truly think we are giving Him our all, but we cannot fully appreciate just how powerful Self is. It cannot be dealt with in a once-and-for-all manner. It requires many seasons of God's dealings for us to see the truth about the Lord, and the truth about ourselves. That is why I say there is more hope for someone who is ready to give up and quit than there is for someone who keeps promising to do better tomorrow. Only after we have tried and failed one hundred, one thousand, or one million times will we at last be able to say, "Lord, I finally understand now that I can originate nothing of my own self, because whenever I do, I meet with nothing but defeat. So I am finished! From now on not my will, but Your Will be done!"

These words are not uttered easily. Anyone can mouth these words and give their mental assent to them, but their behavior all too often contradicts their confession. So the Lord must labor long and hard to work this into us as a heart-attitude and not just lip service. Many Christians wonder why their circumstances are so difficult. They wonder why things never seem to go their way. They wonder why everything seems to rise up and challenge them. At the risk of oversimplifying, let me say that the primary reason for this is that the Lord intends to reduce you to Himself and make you His prisoner.

As the prisoners of the Lord we have no control over our environment, our going out, or our coming in. The truth is that control is an illusion. The Wind blows where He wishes (not where we wish), and you cannot tell where He is coming from or where He is going (cf. Jn. 3:8). So often we think we have God, the Bible, the church, and our Christian life all figured out. We have an answer for every situation. We have a solution for every problem. Suddenly the Wind shifts, and we realize we know nothing at all. We learn that we do not move the Wind, but the Wind moves us. This is God's way of decreasing us and increasing Christ. We learn from experience that "apart from Me, you can do nothing" (Jn. 15:5b).

Increased Difficulties Indicative of Spiritual Maturity

> If anyone would come after me, let him deny himself and take up his cross daily and follow me. (Lk. 9:23).

The Cross explains why things seem to get increasingly difficult for us the farther down the Narrow Path we go. Assuming we are not living in sin and our heart is right before God, when we no longer

The Prisoners of the Lord

"feel" as we once did, does it mean something is wrong? Many Christians would answer yes, something must be wrong. Should we then ask the Lord to restore our good feelings? Again, many Christians, misled into thinking that the Christian life should be one continuous string of mountain-top experiences, would say yes. On the contrary, we should realize that the Lord intends for us to walk by faith, and this is contrary to walking by how we feel.

In order to teach us, the Lord frequently permits us to have a number of spiritual experiences in the beginning of our training. Or, we may hear His voice plainly telling us what to do and where to go. This, of course, is necessary for children who cannot know otherwise. But over time these experiences become less and less frequent. Why? Because He wishes for us to walk with Him without the benefit of a spiritual experience or a good feeling or a clear voice. Now, in order to walk with Him, we must learn to do so based on relationship.

Here is the problem with walking by feelings. If I feel spiritual today, then I will pray, sing, read the Scriptures, and witness with great fervor. But if I feel unspiritual today, then I will do nothing. If this is how we live then we should see that it does not matter whether our feelings are good or bad, or if they result in good works or no works. Either way, we are still living based on how we feel and not based on our union with Christ. Even my "good works" if solely motivated by how I feel, are rooted in Self. They are just as self-centered as my evil works. My feelings, whether they are good, bad, or indifferent, are in the domain of Self, and Self with all its feelings must be delivered over to death. It does not mean a Christian should be totally devoid of feeling, but it means a disciple of the Lord is not ruled by feeling.

This is the practical application of the Cross. Only prisoners carry the Cross – "free" men do not. Those who love themselves will never take it up, for it means you have the sentence of Death in you. Obviously this does not "feel" good, so those who live by how they feel will find it unbearable. It is intended to bring my life to an end so that I may pass through death and come onto Resurrection ground. This is the purpose of all God's dealings with us as disciples. The sooner we become the Lord's prisoner, the sooner we will see His purpose realized in us.

Becoming the Lord's Prisoner

What does it mean to be the prisoner of the Lord? *First*, and foremost, it means giving up our freedom. It means we are no longer free to dress ourselves and go where we please. Others may be able to do as they like, but prisoners of the Lord are not free to do as they like. Others may be able to press ahead no matter what, but all our times and movements are in His hands.

Second, being the prisoner of the Lord means we must accept lengthy periods of solitude. We welcome opportunities for fellowship and friendship when those opportunities present themselves, but as the Lord's prisoner we are frequently asked to be alone and shut up with God. All our relationships must have the imprint of the Cross upon them. That is, we give our friends and our family over to God and receive them back from Him again. In this way the Lord maintains His preeminence.

Third, to be the prisoner of the Lord means that we accept the sentence of death and are resigned to our fate. We are not the Lord's prisoner if we are still protesting our innocence. If we do not agree with the Lord that Self is worthy of death then we unnecessarily delay the inevitable. If we must take up the Cross and be crucified, it is better to submit ourselves to it as Christ did, giving up our spirit into the Father's hands, and bowing our head in peace. So let us drink the Cup that the Father gives us. If we struggle and protest, like the two thieves, then we only prolong our agony, and the soldiers must come and break our legs. Either way, the Cross means death. The sooner we surrender to it the sooner we find Resurrection.

It is a glorious thing to be the prisoner of the Lord, for in our bonds we find liberty. In our weakness we find strength. In our foolishness we find wisdom. In our poverty we find prosperity. By losing everything we find everything. By giving up all things we inherit all things. By accepting the sentence of death we find the Life of the Lord. Let us stretch forth our hands and allow Him to dress us and lead us where He wishes us to go, in the way we would not choose for ourselves, for that is the Narrow Way, and it is the path of blessing, though it be disguised. May the Lord confirm this word to our hearts. Amen.

"Christianity without discipleship is always Christianity without Christ."

~ Dietrich Bonhoeffer

Chapter Ten

The Way of the Cross

"But put on the Lord Jesus Christ, and make no provision for the flesh, to gratify its desires." (Romans 13:14)

"There is a way that seems right to a man, but its end is the way to death." (Proverbs 16:25)

"For the gate is narrow and the way is hard that leads to life, and those who find it are few." (Matthew 7:14)

"I am the Way, and the Truth, and the Life." (John 14:6a)

We talk about "one way" but there are really two ways: the broad way which many take, ending in Death; and the narrow way which a few take, ending in Life. There are two ways presented to us. One way is of man and seems right in man's opinion, but leads to death. The other way is of God and seems wrong in man's opinion, but leads to Life.

We find that Christ is the Way to Life, and He Himself is Life. He is both the means towards the End, as well as the End.

What is God after? What does He seek from us? What does He want? First and foremost, He desires a people who will be conformed to the image of His Son, that they may demonstrate the preeminence of Christ in all things. But how does He gain such a people for Himself? The first step is to reveal His Son to us. This is the narrow gate. We cannot begin to walk the narrow path until we have entered the narrow gate.

Upon entering the narrow gate God begins to change us from the inside out so that it is Christ expressing Himself through us. "Not I, but Christ" (Gal. 2:20ff). This is the narrow path. This narrow path we call discipleship. It leads us somewhere. A path is not for standing still. It has a destination. Where does the path lead? What is the End? Christ as All in All. That is the End. All things work together according to this supreme purpose, His Purpose.

What is a disciple? A disciple is someone who applies their energies to learn a special discipline under a master teacher. There is no other way to be a disciple. There must be a pupil who is taught, and there must be a teacher who teaches. The disciple lives with the teacher, eats and drinks with the teacher, travels about with the teacher, observes the teacher during the course of the day and night, asks a lot of questions and listens intently to the answers. This is the Eastern way of making disciples, and it is the way the Lord Jesus discipled the Twelve.

Disciples sit under the teacher – literally at his feet – and hang on his every word. Disciples memorize their master's teaching and repeat it verbatim to one another, using the same hand gestures, phraseology, and emphasis, until they sound and act just like their teacher. So when you see a mature disciple you will, in essence, see the teacher as well. When the disciple speaks, it is as if the teacher is speaking. This not only honors the teacher but preserves the teaching.

A disciple of the Lord Jesus is someone who enters the narrow gate and walks the narrow path until they come to the end of the narrow path and are left with nothing but Christ. As you can see, this is a very, very narrow way, which is why few find it, and fewer still remain on it once they find it. Nothing of Self can be retained. All of Self must be lost in order to gain Christ.

As we walk the narrow way we are being changed from glory to glory. Today we should reflect a little more of the glory of God than yesterday; tomorrow we will reflect yet more than we did today. This is spiritual growth. Spiritual growth is not more knowledge or increase of years: it is simply more of Him and less of me. He increases as I decrease. This is what it means to be a disciple.

What God Wants is Disciples

God does not want ministers or workers to begin with. We think these things are very important, for how can the Body of Christ get along without ministers and workers? What else does God want if not ministers and workers? Quite simply, He wants disciples first and foremost. There are many ministers and workers today and very few disciples. Everyone either has a ministry or wants a ministry. Everyone is expected to be a minister or a worker. We do not hear too much about being a disciple, yet this is what God must have before He can have anything else in the Ekklesia.

Jesus said go into all the world and make disciples. It is not that ministers and workers are unimportant; indeed they are. But what is the priority? Can a man or a woman truly be a minister or worker on behalf of the Kingdom if they are not a disciple first? Of course not. They can minister and work themselves to death and still be in the flesh, doing many mighty works in the name of Jesus and not know Him at all.

"Those who find it are few." But doesn't everyone know the Way by now? Surely multitudes of people will find it? Not at all. The Way that leads to Life is narrow, and those who find it are few. Isn't "the Way" Jesus? And doesn't everyone know that? Well, everyone has been told that, and they think they know it, but Jesus as He really is and Jesus as He is commonly taught, are two different things.

What is our idea of discipleship? I hear brothers and sisters say, "I have been sitting under the ministry of brother so-and-so for years now." They say this with great pride as if it is something others should be impressed by. I ask them, "How long have you lived with your teacher?" Invariably you discover they do not live with their teacher at all. They simply listen to his sermons in church or on television or on cassette tape or disks. They have no personal relationship with their teacher. In many cases they have never even met in person, much less shared a meal with them.

The Way of the Cross

Be careful whom you "sit under" for you will become just like them, and you will never advance beyond them. Please understand that the Lord did not call us to go forth mentoring and being mentored. A mentor is a synonym for a teacher, guide, or counselor. If I am not mistaken (and I am not), the Holy Spirit is our Teacher, Guide, and Counselor, not man. This is where so many of us have missed it. We are still looking for man – flesh and blood – to affirm us and tell us what to do. Should we encourage one another? Yes. Should we seek advice and prayers of other brothers and sisters? Absolutely. But that does not mean we need a mentor or a "spiritual father" to tell us what to do. Who tells the mentor what to do? His mentor? And who tells the mentor's mentor what to do? You see that this can become ridiculous, and it has in fact become that ridiculous in recent years right up until this present time.

There are people out there who are eager and willing to be your mentor, to teach you how to release your "gifts" or find your place in "ministry" or move in the "prophetic" or pastor a large "church." Anyone who is eager to mentor someone doesn't know himself well enough. Anyone seeking a mentor doesn't know the Master well enough. Finding a mentor isn't difficult. The difficult part is understanding that discipleship has nothing to do with finding a mentor or sitting under a teacher on this earth. Instead the Bible tells us that we have no need of any man to teach us, for the Anointing (Christ) will teach us all things and will lead us into all Truth (1 Jn. 2:27). A teacher who is teaching in the name of Christ will always teach you away from himself and towards Christ as the Teacher. "Less of me and more of Him." Does your mentor do this? Does your pastor do this? Or do they find ways to keep you dependent upon them and their teaching?

Who is Your Teacher?

When the Lord revealed Himself to me I realized that such experiential, intimate knowledge cannot be found in a book, or I would have had it years ago. It cannot be found simply by reading the Bible, or everyone who has a Bible would know the Truth experientially, and we know that is simply not the case. It is a revelation of Truth as a Person, not as a philosophy, and from that day forward I understood that man cannot add to it or take away anything from it. That is when I stopped seeking the affirmation or confirmation of man.

I understood then (for the first time) that there is only one Teacher, and I am His disciple. I do not belong to anyone else, and no one else belongs to me. This was not something I would have understood automatically. As a pastor I was used to talking about "my sheep" and "my congregation" and "my church" as if I owned something. But when I discovered that there is One Flock guided by One Shepherd I knew then that I owned no one, and no one owned me. I belonged to Him, and they belonged to Him. What liberty! For me certainly, but more so, for the ones who were formerly "sitting under my teaching." People would come to me to be taught instead of to others, because they claimed they could not be fed by others, only by me. What a tragedy! Who is your source? Where did the manna come from? From Moses? No, "it was not Moses who gave you the bread from heaven, but My Father gives you the true bread from heaven." (Jn. 6:32). When will we look away from Moses the man, towards Christ the Living Bread?

Now I can say (and indeed, "boast" is not too strong of a word here) that my teaching is not my own. It is from Christ, for Christ, and unto Christ as All in All. My boast is that my teaching does not come from a human source. That is not to say that I have not learned much from the likes of Watchman Nee, T. Austin-Sparks, and others. I have read their writings for years and continue to read them. But what I know, I did not learn in a book. I do not read them to discover something new, but to verify something I already know. We have the same Teacher.

What is my point? To boast of myself? Not at all, but to boast of my Teacher! There is no better thing in the world than to have someone ask, "Where did you learn what you know? Who taught you these things?" and for you to respond, "Jesus Christ is my Teacher, and He taught me everything I know." This is discipleship! The Lord told us to call no earthly man "Rabbi" (that is, Teacher) because you only have One Teacher (Mt. 23:8,9). But how many of us can say that?

Become His disciple. Sit at His feet and hear His Word. There is no other way to learn. You cannot get it from someone else; you must get it from Him. He is Truth.

The Cost of Discipleship

What does it cost to become a disciple of the Lord Jesus Christ? What does one have to give up? There is truly only one thing that must be given up. It is not, and it never has been, a question of giving up friends, family, material possessions, fame and fortune. You can give up all those things, just like the first disciples of the Lord, and still run away and deny Him.

Forget the outward things and go right to the heart of the matter. Only one thing is necessary, and if we give up this one thing then we are qualified to be disciples of the Lord. What is the one thing? All we have to give up is our way.

There are two ways: one that seems right, and one that is right. One is my way, the other is His way.

Yes, if we are willing to give up our way then we have, in effect, given up everything. I am thinking of a dear man who pastors a church, but he does it according to his way. Unfortunately he cannot see that he is pastoring according to his way. Not that his way is necessarily bad, because there is a lot of good work in his ministry. But it is not purely the Way of Christ. I do not expect that he will give up his church, or his ministry. The reality is that he will probably never give up his work. The glorious thing is he does not have to give up a single thing, except his own way! If he will but give that up, everything else will take care of itself. The same is true of us.

That is not to say that we will keep everything. When we give up our way then we will, in fact, lose quite a bit. We will lose the admiration and appreciation of the world. We will lose the prestige and position we once enjoyed. We may very well lose friends and even members of our family who will not approve of us anymore.

The disciple is not greater than the Master, but it is enough for the disciple to be like the Master. The cost is great, but the reward is greater. "He is no fool who gives what he cannot keep in order to gain what he cannot lose."

"The Christian life is not by effort, and not by struggle; not merely by trying to put into practice certain maxims, or by trying to attain to a certain measure; but from beginning to end, and all together, it is a matter of knowing the Lord Jesus within."

~ T. Austin-Sparks

Chapter Eleven

Embrace the Cross

"Can I accept Jesus as Savior, but not accept Him as Lord? Can I receive salvation, but not discipleship?"

Many, in their haste to defend the fact that they are "saved by grace" and not by works, believe that it is perfectly acceptable to accept Jesus as Savior and ignore or procrastinate every instruction He gives. Loving God, loving your neighbor, taking up the Cross, following Jesus, obeying His commands – all of this (they say) is for older, more experienced Christians, and are not conditions of being saved at all. Since we are "under grace" (so the thinking goes) discipleship is optional, but not mandatory. There is (they believe) really nothing more to being saved than to simply repeat the Sinner's Prayer.

It is certainly true that we are not saved by earning our salvation through good works and deeds. We are saved by grace, through faith, and it is the gift of God (cf. Eph. 2:8). But it is also true that, while works do not "save" us, works certainly do indicate that we have been saved. An orange tree is an orange tree as soon as it is planted, even before it produces fruit. It is not an orange tree because it produces oranges; it produces oranges because it is an orange tree. The fruit is the evidence of what it already is. If it were to suddenly produce rotten apples then we know for certain that it is not what we thought it was.

The one who has really been saved will produce "much fruit" (Jn. 15:8) and will "walk worthy" of their calling (Eph. 4:1). That is to say, the evidence of a "born again" person is not in what they say they believe, but in how they actually live. Even the phrase "born again" indicates more than just a change of heart; it represents a spiritual death, burial, and resurrection; a new life. Thus, no one can be truly "born again" until and unless they embrace the Cross, die with Christ, and are raised to Life in Him.

What does the Scripture say about this? "Not everyone who says to me, 'Lord, Lord,' will enter the kingdom of heaven, but the one who does the will of my Father who is in heaven" (Mt. 7:21). This should lay to rest the false premise that merely calling Jesus "Lord" is sufficient without some very real evidence to back up that confession. It is not those who *say*, but those who *do*; not mere *believers*, but those who *put into practice*. Jesus said that those who hear His teachings *and put them into practice* are like the wise man who built his house on the rock; but those who only hear and do *not* put them into practice are like the foolish man who built his house on the sand (cf. Mt. 7:24-27).

Abraham Lincoln once asked his cabinet members, "If we call a tail a leg, how many legs does a dog have?" The president's counselors considered it and replied, "If we call a tail a leg, then a dog has five legs." Lincoln shook his head. "No. A dog has four legs. Calling a tail a leg doesn't make it so." In the same way, calling Jesus "Lord" does not necessarily mean you have submitted to His Lordship. The proof of His Lordship over you is not in what you call Him; it is in the obedience to what He says.

Then there is the often-quoted passage in Romans, where Paul declares that "if you confess with your mouth that Jesus is Lord and believe in your heart that God raised him from the dead, you will be saved." (Rom. 10:9). This seems fairly straightforward. Where is discipleship mentioned at all? It appears that a simple confession and belief is enough. Yet, as we have already seen, confessing Jesus as Lord is only valid if there is obedience to what the Lord says. How interesting that Paul does not say you are saved by confessing that Jesus is *Savior*, but by confessing that Jesus is *Lord*. Discipleship is implied within the confession of Lordship; if I really confess Jesus as Lord, and really believe that He is Lord, then I will naturally *do* the things my Lord commands. The Master looks not at the words, but at the actions.

Jesus said to go into all the world and make *disciples*, not *decisions*. But it is much easier to record *decisions* for Christ than it is to make *disciples* for Christ. And so the modern church asks people to simply "confess Jesus as your personal Savior" – something unknown to the early believers, who were taught to confess Jesus as *Lord* and then backup their confession with tangible evidence of a changed life.

The rich young ruler came to Jesus looking for "eternal life." Jesus could have very easily said, "I am the Life" and led him in a prayer. Instead, Jesus offered the man something he really wasn't looking for: a Cross.

Have you considered that Jesus never did lead anyone in a prayer to be saved? He simply said, "Follow Me." What can "follow Me" mean if it does not mean following Him to the Cross, and experiencing death and resurrection? Taking up the Cross and following Jesus is how a person is *saved*. There is no other way. Even when Jesus refers to Himself as the "Way" this implies a Path, a certain manner of life, some kind of journey that has a starting point and a finishing point. This Way is the Difficult Path that comes after the Narrow Gate (see Mt. 7:14). This Way is discipleship, which is nothing more than a progressive learning to give up my way for His Way and my own Self-life for His Life. The Cross represents this continual death to Self so that a new Life, a new way of living, a new way of being, can come forth.

Jesus never made a distinction between being saved and being a disciple. He is not "Savior" for new Christians and "Lord" for older, more deeply committed Christians. Either He is Lord *of* all, or He isn't Lord *at* all.

Discipleship: The Narrow Path

"Do not speak of discipleship when you give the altar call," the modern church teaches. "You just catch the fish and let Jesus clean them. If you try to make too many demands on people before they get saved then you might scare them away." This certainly sounds reasonable, but if this is correct advice then it makes you wonder why Jesus, the Ultimate Fisher of Men, would say things like this:

> Whoever loves father or mother more than me is not worthy of me, and whoever loves son or daughter more than me is not worthy of me. And whoever does not take his cross and follow me is not worthy of me. Whoever finds his life will lose it, and whoever loses his life for my sake will find it. (Mt. 10:37-39)

> And [Jesus] called to him the crowd with his disciples and said to them, "If anyone would come after me, let him deny himself and take up his cross and follow me." (Mk. 8:34)

> And [Jesus] said to all, "If anyone would come after me, let him deny himself and take up his cross daily and follow me. For whoever would save his life will lose it, but whoever loses his life for my sake will save it." (Lk. 9:23,24)

> To another [Jesus] said, "Follow me." But he said, "Lord, let me first go and bury my father." And Jesus said to him, "Leave the dead to bury their own dead. But as for you, go and proclaim the kingdom of God." Yet another said, "I will follow you, Lord, but let me first say farewell to those at my home." Jesus said to him, "No one who puts his hand to the plow and looks back is fit for the kingdom of God." (Lk. 9:59-62)

> If anyone comes to me and does not hate his own father and mother and wife and children and brothers and sisters, yes, and even his own life, he cannot be my disciple. Whoever does not bear his own cross and come after me cannot be my disciple. For which of you, desiring to build a tower, does not first sit down and count the cost, whether he has enough to complete it? ...So therefore, any one of you who does not renounce all that he has cannot be my disciple. (Lk. 14:26-28,33)

> Whoever loves his life loses it, and whoever hates his life in this world will keep it for eternal life. (Jn. 12:25)

If Jesus (or anyone else) gave an altar call like this, no one would come forward. When was the last time a preacher told someone they have to hate their life in this world in order to keep it for eternity?

As hard as these words of Jesus are, wisdom is justified by the fruit it produces. The kind of fruit you get is determined by the kind of seeds you plant. You get exactly what you ask for. If you preach an easy message and invite someone to pray an easy prayer and they become an easy believer in an easy Jesus, then you get millions of fair-weather, lukewarm, self-centered "converts" who fall away at the first sign of difficulty. On the other hand, twelve men who learned to be completely surrendered to the difficult, "unrealistic" demands of discipleship managed to "turn the world upside down" (Acts 17:6).

Embrace the Cross

When the British explorer Ernest Shackleton needed men to accompany him on his first expedition to Antarctica, he allegedly placed the following classified advertisement in the newspaper:

MEN WANTED FOR HAZARDOUS JOURNEY.
Low wages, bitter cold, long hours
of complete darkness. Safe return doubtful.
Honour and recognition in event of success.

This "invitation" did not bring many responses, but the few men who did respond were exactly the kind Shackleton wanted. Likewise, Jesus knows exactly the kind of disciple He wants, and He knows exactly how to ask for them. There is great joy in following Jesus, and the possibility of ruling and reigning with Him in His Kingdom is certainly appealing. But following Jesus is not easy. Taking up the Cross is difficult.

Of course, there is another way. The Easy Path that "many find" (Mt. 7:13) makes discipleship into an option for those who get serious later on. Ironically, those who take the Easy Path in the beginning never really "get serious" later. Why should they? There is no expectation, no hard sayings, no Cross to embrace daily, no difficult demands or need for self-denial – and so there is no spiritual growth, no maturity, or deep knowledge of God. This Easy Path leads to destruction. Could it be that "the many" who take the Easy Path are all the while calling Jesus "Lord, Lord" but not actually *doing* what He says?

The Way of the Cross is a narrow way, a difficult way, but a necessary way if we ever intend to find Life.

Entering the Gate is not the end of the journey, it is the beginning of the journey. It is at the end of the Path that one finds Life (Mt. 7:14), not the beginning.

Why Discipleship is Difficult

Following Jesus is synonymous with embracing the Cross, and embracing the Cross is the only way a person can experience the saving power of Christ:

> "I know very well how foolish the message of the cross sounds to those who are on the road to destruction. But we who are being saved recognize this message as the very power of God. (1 Cor. 1:18, NLT)

If we have eternal life at all it is because we have been crucified, dead, buried, and resurrected with Christ. This is what it means to be "saved." It is not the praying of a prayer, only to go out and continue living as if nothing has ever happened; or to pray a prayer and then mark it off our spiritual "to do" list. If we are truly saved then we will continue to follow Him: "Therefore, as you received Christ Jesus the Lord, so walk in him, rooted and built up in him and established in the faith, just as you were taught, abounding in thanksgiving" (Col. 2:6,7). This is the Narrow Path of discipleship.

Why is it difficult? It is not difficult in the sense that *religion* is difficult. Discipleship does not refer to the crushing burden of religious legalism and snobbery, maintaining a "holier-than-thou" appearance, joining the local religious establishment, succumbing to the dreaded "death-by-church-volunteerism", trying to measure up in God's eyes, trying to please other people, or maintaining rigid conformity to external rules and regulations designed to keep you "sanctified." Thank God, following Jesus has nothing to do with being religious!

The difficulty of discipleship is that we are being led and taught by One whose thoughts and ways are higher than our own. We can see this difficulty in the earthly disciples of Jesus. He was clearly from another world. His thoughts, His actions, His reasoning, His way of looking at people and things, were almost always the opposite of what the disciples thought. They looked, but He *saw*. And they had a hard time seeing things as He saw them. That is the difficulty you and I also experience as we try to follow Him. Before any learning can happen there is a great deal of *unlearning* that must take place.

Moses is a good example of this. Israel's future deliverer spent the first forty years of his life living as a prince in Egypt. At the end of forty years, the Bible says, "Moses was instructed in all the wisdom of the Egyptians, and he was mighty in his words and deeds" (Acts 7:22). At this point, most would say that Moses was qualified to lead his people out of Egypt. Yet when he attempted to lead them, he completely failed. Instead God drew Moses out into the desert to learn His ways. But in order to learn the ways of God, Moses had to *unlearn* the ways of the Egyptians. This took yet another forty years of training. Moses had tied himself up into a great big knot that had to be untangled. Finally, at the age of eighty years old, God knew that Moses was ready even though Moses himself now thought he was not ready; and it was then that God sent him back to Egypt to lead the people out.

That is how the Cross works: unlearning our way and learning His way. Could we surrender to a process that might take eighty years to complete? Letting go of our own ways in order to learn the ways of Another is easier said than done. The natural, easiest path is to revert back to what we already know, because even if what we already know is inferior, at least it is predictable and relatively safe.

The Cross brings us face-to-face with our own weakness, our own inability, our own lack of knowing. These are not pleasant things for anyone to experience. It wounds our pride. It makes us feel uncomfortable. It makes us look like a failure sometimes. It does not help us to win the applause and the praise of others; just the opposite, in fact. It makes us feel inadequate.

But the truth is that we really *are* inadequate. The Cross is not telling us any new truth, it is simply revealing what has been true all along: that "apart from [Christ] you can do nothing" (Jn. 15:5). The Cross brings us face-to-face with who we really are apart from Jesus, and who we really are apart from Him is a rotten, stinking mess. "For I know that nothing good dwells in me, that is, in my flesh" (Rom. 7:18a). Paul *knew* this because he *knew* the Cross. Do we know it? Those who embrace the Cross have acknowledged this in themselves and have surrendered their way over to His Way.

The Essence of Embracing the Cross: Surrender

In what areas must we acknowledge this inability to do anything apart from Christ? It must not only be acknowledged: it must be truly seen, deeply felt, and painfully experienced in *every* area of our life, one step at a time. This is the work of the Cross. In our daily life we come up against situations that we cannot overcome in our own strength, or with our own wisdom. We need a strength and a wisdom that comes from Above, that comes from Beyond, that comes from Another outside of us and yet rises up from within us.

If you are truly born-again then you have experienced this at least *once* in your life, in at least *one area* of your life. At least once you have come to recognize your inability to save yourself, and so you surrendered to Christ and trusted Jesus to do in you and through you what you could not do on your own. That surrender was, in essence, "taking up the Cross" with respect to your salvation. I have died to saving myself. I cannot save myself; and since I cannot, I will not. I will only trust in the Life of the Lord to do what I have (at last!) learned that I cannot do. This is what is means to "embrace the Cross" in the area of salvation. And we see that when the death to Self is thorough and complete – that is, when we stop trying to save ourselves and cast ourselves upon the grace of God, then God raises us from the dead. That which was impossible before is now accomplished by God. We are thankful recipients of His grace, and He receives all the praise and the glory since we have done nothing and He has done everything. This is the principle of the Cross.

It does not matter what your situation is; the Cross is sufficient. If the Cross is the power of God for salvation, then the Cross is also the power of God for your relationships, your spiritual growth and development, your life's purpose, your encouragement and strength, and your victory over everything which hinders and distracts and comes against you. At one time in your life you learned you could not save yourself – that was the work of the Cross. Now, accept the work of the Cross and learn that just as you could not save yourself, neither can you love God, love your neighbor, forgive those who have sinned against you, cast out devils, be a bold witness for Christ, or fulfill your destiny in your own strength. Just as you once relied upon Christ to save you, so now you must rely upon Christ to *live* through you every day. Just as you continually rely upon Christ for salvation, so you must continually rely upon Christ for everything else.

"As you have *received* Christ Jesus the Lord..." That is the Gate. "...So walk in Him." That is the Path. If you can admit defeat, if you can surrender yourself over to God in the area of "salvation" then you can (and should) do the same thing in every other area of your life. Walk in Him as you received Him: by unconditionally surrendering to His Will, His Purpose,

His Power, His Lordship. Embrace the Cross! The sooner the better!

When we cease doing what we cannot do, then He begins to do what we cannot. *This is the fruit produced by those who are truly born again.* Our works are not religious works at all, they are simply the works of Him Who now lives in us. When we cease struggling and surrender to crucifixion then He comes forth in power and glory to raise us from the dead. This is what it means to be a Christian and a disciple of Jesus.

A brother came to me who suffered from a bad habit. He had tried every means known to man to break himself from this habit. No stone was left unturned. First he tried all the "Christian" cures: prayer, fasting, binding and loosing, exorcism, positive confession. He had made vows to God and had threatened himself with dire consequences if he ever broke his vows. But break them he did. When all these attempts to address the problem spiritually failed, he tried some psychological remedies: visualization, counseling, psychotherapy, self-help courses, motivational speakers, natural remedies, prescription drugs. He even wore a rubber band around his wrist so that he could snap it against his skin whenever his thoughts began to go astray. In this way (he had been told) the pain would interrupt his thought patterns and he would "snap" back into reality. He had red welts on his wrist from snapping the rubber band over and over. Obviously the rubber band trick wasn't working. In fact, nothing had worked. This is the condition he was in when he sought me out.

"I have tried everything, and I cannot break this habit! What else can I do?" he asked.

"Let me repeat what I just heard you say," I answered. "You said you cannot break this habit." He nodded. "Then you asked, 'What else can I do?'" He nodded again.

"Listen to what you just said," I replied. "You said, 'I cannot... what else can I do?'" He didn't understand, so I tried again. "What you are saying is, 'I cannot, I cannot, I cannot.' Then, in the same breath, you are asking, 'What else can I do?' And the answer is: nothing. There is nothing else you can do. You have done it all. So if you really believe that you cannot do it then stop *trying* to do it. Every time you try, you are expressing a belief that you still think you can do it. Clearly you cannot."

He thought on this and said, "Yes, but if I stop trying, then it will surely defeat me." I answered, "You are already defeated. Now you must admit your defeat so that you can overcome. What do you have to show for all your trying? Nothing but a series of disappointing failures. Do you see that if you cannot, then all the trying in the world is pointless? If it is impossible for me to lift 1,000 pounds then I should not even attempt it. This habit is 10,000 pounds to you. Can you lift it? No. Do you still think you can? Then God will allow you to keep on trying, and will wait for you to give up trying. Sooner or later you must learn to stop trying to do what you cannot do. The purpose of these multiple failures is to teach you one thing: you *cannot*. If you will learn this lesson then it is worth

Embrace the Cross

failing a thousand times. If you have truly learned it this time then go to God and tell Him that you quit. Tell Him that you have tried to do it your way but you are powerless. Surrender it all to Him. Give up trying and admit that apart from Him it cannot be done. Go to the Cross and die with respect to this thing and see what God does with it." He thought on this and wanted to disagree but his experience had proved that the more he tried the more often he failed.

Then something happened. He finally saw that there was no use in trying to do what he could not do. "I cannot," he said, "Therefore, I *will* not!" A new hope had dawned within him: he saw that "What is impossible with men is possible with God" (Lk. 18:27). But now he understood that in order for God to do what is *impossible* for man to do, man must first realize that it is *impossible* for man to do it! He saw for the first time that God can do more for him in five seconds of "giving up" than he could do for himself through a whole lifetime of "trying."

So together we prayed, and his prayer went something like this: "Today, Lord, I am finished. I give up. I have tried everything and nothing has worked. This is impossible with me, but not with You. With You all things are possible! Therefore, I trust You to do what I cannot do. If you do it then I will overcome; if You do not do it then I will forever be defeated. Just as I trust in You to save me, so I trust in You to overcome this thing. I cannot, but You can." Without realizing it, this brother had *embraced the Cross*. He "died" to all his efforts and God "raised him from the dead" with a tremendous deliverance.

Embracing the Cross is not a once-and-for-all act, but a daily attitude of knowing our insufficiency in order to know the sufficiency of Christ. Jesus asks us to take up the Cross "daily" (Lk. 9:23) and Paul said "I die daily" (1 Cor. 15:31). Since we daily meet with temptations, tests and trials, so we must daily affirm and reaffirm who we are in Christ: the crucified, dead, buried, resurrected, ascended and seated Branches of the crucified, dead, buried, resurrected, ascended, and seated Vine. As disciples, we take up the Cross daily, which means we are always in a state of surrender and submission to the Lord Jesus, constantly forsaking our own way for His Way. This moment-by-moment yielding to Him is summed up in this saying: "Not I, but Christ" (Gal. 2:20ff).

Here is what this surrender looks like in practical terms.

The Cross and Our Thought Life

> And [Jesus] said to him, "You shall love the Lord your God with all your heart and with all your soul and with all your mind." (Mt. 22:27)

> To set the mind on the flesh is death, but to set the mind on the Spirit is life and peace. (Rom. 8:6)

> Do not be conformed to this world, but be transformed by the renewal of your mind. (Rom. 12:2a)
>
> We have the mind of Christ. (1 Cor. 2:16b)
>
> We destroy arguments and every lofty opinion raised against the knowledge of God, and take every thought captive to obey Christ. (2 Cor. 10:5)
>
> And the peace of God, which surpasses all understanding, will guard your hearts and your minds in Christ Jesus. (Phil. 4:7)

When we embrace the Cross in our thought life we will see that our own thinking is limited, and at times, completely the opposite of God's thoughts. We will readily see that our opinions, our prejudices, our very point of view, all need radical transformation. We will see how untrustworthy and unpredictable our mind, will and emotions can be apart from God.

As we submit ourselves to the Cross we see that God does not turn us into unthinking, unfeeling creatures of wood or stone; instead, He renews and transforms our mind so that our thoughts reflect His thoughts, and our mind reflects His mind. We will no longer be carried away by our emotions or find false comfort in our superior intellect. Our emotions will accurately convey God's own heart – meaning we can rightly "Rejoice with those who rejoice, weep with those who weep" (Rom. 12:15). Our intellect, instead of arguing against God, will be obedient to Christ. Our thoughts will be submitted to His wisdom and will assist us in understanding His Will and His Ways.

The Cross and Our Attitude Towards Sin

The one who embraces the Cross experiences freedom from the *penalty* of sin as well as the *power* of sin. Having been "crucified with Christ" (Gal. 2:20a), the follower of Jesus has already suffered the penalty of sin and been released from any guilt or condemnation because of sin. Perhaps you have noticed, however, that even followers of Jesus, though free from the *penalty* of sin, are not immediately released from the *power* of sin. Just like the brother who tried to free himself from the bad habit, disciples of Jesus often struggle against the seemingly insurmountable power of sin, even though they are free from its penalty.

This is why the Cross must be embraced and taken up *daily* as a principle of living. This is the practical application of taking up the Cross. If we ever lay down the Cross and attempt anything in our own power then we will be defeated. But as we continually reckon ourselves "dead to sin but alive to God through Christ" (Rom. 6:11) then what is true in principle eventually becomes true in our experience: sin begins to lose its power to control us, and we begin to see that we do have a choice. We will begin to see that we are no longer slaves to sin, but "if the Son sets you free, you will be free indeed" (Jn. 8:36).

As we daily embrace the Cross we will discover that the truth of our freedom in Christ becomes more real to us than the sin that used to imprison us. We will learn that the Cross is not a mere theory, philosophy, or theological teaching; the Cross is a very real, practical, spiritual principle of Life overcoming Death, Light overcoming Darkness, and God's Power being revealed in the midst of our weakness.

The Cross and Our Attitude Towards Self

> By the grace of God I am what I am. (1 Cor. 15:10a)

> ...not I, but Christ... (Gal. 2:20ff)

> For we are the real circumcision, who worship by the Spirit of God and glory in Christ Jesus and put no confidence in the flesh. (Phil. 3:3)

> I can do all things through Christ Who strengthens me. (Phil. 4:13)

The Cross helps us to see that the real problem is not what we *do* but what we *are*. Behind the deed is a motive, and that motive is usually self-serving. We begin to see that *we* are the problem.

"Not I, but Christ" is the solution to the problem of Self, and we arrive at this solution by embracing the Cross. The Cross empties us of any illusions about ourselves. We lose all confidence in the flesh. Ironically, this does not leave us empty and worthless, shuffling about with a false humility, protesting that we are nothing but miserable worms. Instead, the Cross removes Self so that Christ can come forth in Resurrection power in us and through us. Only then is the one who can do nothing apart from Christ transformed into a person who can do all things through Him. The key is, of course, that they are now doing all things *through Christ*, and not doing them in their own power or for their own glory.

"By the grace of God, I am what I am." This is the correct way to perceive one's self. In and of myself, I am nothing, and can do nothing; but by the grace of God, I am what I am, and with His power I can do anything. Of course, only the crucified can make such a statement. For those who have not embraced the Cross this sounds like a lot of bluster and foolish boasting. There is a fine line between self-esteem and Christ-esteem, and the words sometimes sound the same. But those who know the Cross know the difference between self-centered pride and Christ-centered passion.

The Cross and Our Attitude Towards Satan

> I have given you authority to tread on serpents and scorpions, and over all the power of the enemy, and nothing shall hurt you. (Lk. 10:19)

> Having disarmed principalities and powers, He made a public spectacle of them, triumphing over them in [the cross]. (Col. 2:15)

> The reason the Son of God appeared was to destroy the works of the devil... (1 Jn. 3:8b)

> They overcame [the dragon] by the blood of the Lamb and by the word of their testimony; they did not love their lives so much as to shrink from death. (Rev. 12:11)

No one can overcome a spiritual adversary unless they embrace the Cross. The ones who overcome the dragon do so by the blood of the Lamb and by not loving their own lives. Their testimony is: "not I, but Christ." The blood, and loving not their life, and their testimony, all point to the same thing: these are people of the Cross. They did not love their own lives, but they gave up their lives; therefore God has raised them from the dead and they have entered into the victory of Christ.

You cannot kill a dead man. You cannot defeat a person who has already died. What more can you do to a man once he has died and been raised to life again? Those who embrace the Cross have inherited the victory of Christ over all the works of the devil. This is the spiritual principle. The practical expression of this principle is seen when I demonstrate this victory in the battles of everyday life. If what God says about us is true, then we are not fighting *for* victory, we are fighting *from* victory – and actually, we not fighting at all; we are merely *standing* in a victory that was given to us in Christ: "Stand therefore" (Eph. 6:14).

In the heat of battle it does not always seem as if the enemy is defeated. Goliath will oppose, curse, and threaten you with all sorts of taunts to convince you that you are defeated. If we listen to him long enough we will begin to doubt and this is enough to cause us to falter. We can simply ignore the lies of the enemy and stand in the truth. Our weapon of choice is the Cross. We simply return to the victory that is ours in Christ and we stand upon that finished work, and every time we do so, we demonstrate its power.

Without the Cross we are naked and unprepared for facing Goliath or anything else that opposes us; but with the Cross we can no more fail than Jesus can fail. "Not I, but Christ" defeats anything and everything that rises up to steal, kill, and destroy. It does not matter if we face Goliath, or a bad habit, or a difficult circumstance, or even the devil himself. Sooner or later, the Cross will shine forth in victory – as long as we embrace it until the very end!

The Cross and Our Attitude Towards the World

> But far be it from me to boast except in the cross of our Lord Jesus Christ, by which the world has been crucified to me, and I to the world. (Gal. 6:14)

> Little children, you are from God and have overcome them, for he who is in you is greater than he who is in the world. (1 Jn. 4:4)

The one who has embraced the Cross can be trusted to live *in* the world without being *of* the world. Followers of Jesus are intended to be the "light of the world" (Mt. 5:14). How can we be the light of the world if we are forever tempted by the world and the things of the world? God desires a crucified people who can represent Him in the earth and be faithful to Him even in the midst of a dark, rebellious world.

Jesus prayed for His disciples: "I do not ask that you take them out of the world, but that you keep them from evil" (Jn. 17:15). This prayer of Jesus is answered when we embrace the Cross. The Cross renders us dead to the world so that we can bring Life to others who are in the world and not worry that we may become contaminated or polluted by the things we encounter.

Jesus was not afraid of being around sinners. He affected them for good, and they were powerless to affect Him for evil. This same Jesus lives within us, and He is greater than anything we may encounter in the world. So if we are to follow His example then we must be as dead to the things of the world as He was. How is this accomplished? God's solution is for us to embrace the Cross so that we can be truly "dead" to the world's temptations and "alive" to Him.

The Cross and Our Attitude Towards "Ministry"

Often, those who believe they are called by God to some kind of ministry represent a significant challenge. Most of them are very gifted and talented. Many of them start out with a good heart and have a genuine desire to serve God and help others. But they also usually have an ambition and a desire to be seen, heard, and approved by men. Eventually the "ministry" becomes a means through which "serving God" becomes a pretext for serving Self, or serving God and Self at the same time. If these selfish ambitions have not been delivered over to the Cross then it represents an impure mixture that God cannot endorse.

Keith Green was already a talented musician and recording artist before he met Christ. It would be natural to assume that God would now use his musical gifts in some ministry capacity. With characteristic zeal and enthusiasm, Keith plunged into the world of the Christian music industry. But eventually he discovered that in order for God to truly use his music, the old Keith Green would have to die; the gift, the talents, the ability that he brought with him into the Kingdom of God had to go through the Cross before God could use them. He embraced the Cross and put aside the piano for a period of months, saying he would never take it up again unless God allowed him to.

One night, after being asked to play at a charity benefit, he reluctantly agreed. About halfway through the song, a pronounced change came over him, and afterwards he told his wife, "I believe that God gave me my music back tonight." From there, Keith Green's music and ministry grew and touched the lives of millions of people before his life was cut short in a plane crash. But long before Keith died in that accident, he "died" on the Cross, and that's why his ministry continues to produce Life today. He discovered it really wasn't "his" music after all; it was God's.

To deliver your ministry over to the Cross and allow it to be crucified is a difficult thing. It represents Isaac, the very thing that God has promised, the thing you love the most, the thing you would give your life for. How difficult it was for Abraham to offer up Isaac! But this is the way of the Cross. And do not suppose that once a thing is delivered over to death and then "returned" in resurrection that it is now yours to do with as you please. The mark of the Cross is upon it from that day forward, and it is kept alive by the Life of the Lord. The moment we touch it or take it back into our own power, we remove it from resurrection ground, and it dies. Embracing the Cross *daily* is the only way it can be maintained.

The Purpose of All God's Dealings

We have only touched on a few aspects of how the Cross transforms the disciple of Jesus. Those who embrace the Cross will find that it penetrates deeply, touching every aspect of their life. To the degree that we allow the Cross to do its work in us, to that same degree will we experience the blessing, the freedom, and the power of Resurrection Life. As we are decreased, He is increased (Jn. 3:30). More of Jesus and less of me: this is the Narrow Path, the path of discipleship, the way of spiritual growth and maturity.

You may have prayed a prayer; but have you embraced the Cross? You may have walked the aisle and joined a church; but have you embraced the Cross?

You may be the most faithful, devout, dedicated church attender and supporter; but have you embraced the Cross? You may be the most wretched sinner and feel unworthy of any good thing; but have you embraced the Cross?

The Cross does not discriminate between good or bad, worthy or unworthy, righteous or unrighteous, young or old, male or female, Jew or Gentile – the Way is the same, and the words of the Master are simple and straightforward to one and to all: *Follow Me*. It doesn't matter how good or bad we think we are, whether we are religious or irreligious, whether we are rich or poor; saint and sinner alike must embrace the Cross and lose their old life in order to find their new life: *in Him*.

Are You Ready to Take the Next Step?

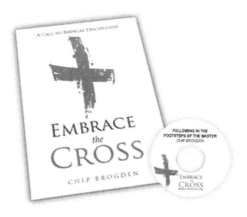

You've read the book. Now, put what you've read to use! Our *free* Basic Discipleship Challenge is a simple, easy-to-understand training program designed to get your spiritual life *on track* and *on target*. It's a great way for you to start (or re-start) your Christian walk in a Christ-centered direction and stay focused on *relationship* - not religion!

To find out more, visit:
EmbraceTheCross.Org
Sponsored by TheSchoolofChrist.Org

To contact the author, obtain additional copies of this book, or request a complete listing of books, audio teachings, and other resources available, please visit our website.

TheSchoolOfChrist.Org

Made in the USA
Lexington, KY
06 July 2015